Greentailing and Other Revolutions in Retail

Greentailing and Other Revolutions in Retail

Hot Ideas That Are Grabbing Customers' Attention and Raising Profits

Neil Z. Stern
Willard N. Ander

WILEY

John Wiley & Sons, Inc.

Published by John Wiley & Sons, Inc., Hoboken, New Jersey.
Published simultaneously in Canada.

For general information on our other products and services or for technical
support, please contact our Customer Care Department within the United States
at (800) 762-2974, outside the United States at (317) 572-3993 or fax (317) 572-4002.

Wiley also publishes its books in a variety of electronic formats. Some content that
appears in print may not be available in electronic books. For more information
about Wiley products, visit our web site at www.wiley.com.

Library of Congress Cataloging-in-Publication Data:

Stern, Neil Z.
    Greentailing and other revolutions in retail : hot ideas that are grabbing
customers' attention and raising profits/Neil Z. Stern, Willard N. Ander.
        p. cm.
    Includes bibliographical references and index.
    ISBN 978-0-470-28858-0 (cloth)
1. Retail trade–Management.   I. Ander, Willard N.   II. Title.
    HF5429.S734 2008
    658.8'7–dc22

                                                                2008012263

Printed in the United States of America.

10 9 8 7 6 5 4 3 2 1

Contents

Preface

You say you want a revolution.
Well, you know we all want to change the world.[1]
                                                    —*The Beatles*

Symbolically, we chose to begin writing *Green-tailing and Other Revolutions in Retailing* on November 23, 2007. That day was better known in retail circles as "Black Friday," the day after Thanksgiving, and the supposed start of the holiday shopping season. It received the name Black Friday years ago for also being the day that retailers finally begin to reap profits after losing money for the majority of the year. For many years, it was also the biggest shopping day in terms of overall sales, with cash registers merrily ringing away. Though Black Friday has long since lost its distinction as the biggest shopping day (procrastinating shoppers have turned the weekend before Christmas into the biggest shopping period), sales on Black Friday for 2007 were still estimated to be well over $10 billion.

Retailers are no longer content to simply wait for Black Friday to kick off the holiday season. Many retailers simply blur the lines between holidays, with Christmas products for sale even before Halloween ends. With the holiday season so important to retailers, the sooner they can get sales, the reasoning goes, the better. Nor, seemingly, can they wait to open their doors. A quick perusal of the dozens of holiday ads spread out in front of us show that 4:00 AM seems to be the "right" time to start sales. If you're not an early riser, no problem—most stores also managed to stay open until midnight. And more stores still offered promotions that kept them open during the holidays for days *and* nights. For those customers sleep deprived enough to show up at those early bird sales, fantastic bargains awaited: 42" HD plasma TVs were being sold in some stores for under $1,000—the same item was well over $5,000 just two years ago. Vacuum cleaners were being sold for $25 and brand name jeans for $9. Could there be any truer indication that America's frenzy for the pursuit of more for less continues unabated?

Indeed, a simplistic but startlingly accurate view of retailing over the past 100 years or so reveals that almost all retail innovation can be directly traced to the retailer's constant quest to determine ways to sell products for less, and the consumer's eagerness to embrace this philosophy. And, by selling products for less money, we entice consumers to buy more. This has meant wondrous innovation on both the supply and demand side of the equation. From a supply standpoint, sophisticated logistics and distribution, enormous advances in technology help to manage the business in a smarter manner, and the globalization of sourcing has helped keep costs (and subsequent prices to the consumer) low.

From a demand side, there has been a constant evolution (and sometimes revolution) from a format standpoint. The development of the self-service supermarket (along with the development of the shopping cart) and the invention and evolution of the discount store and the Internet have changed the way Americans shop. New formats have come along, all figuring out a way to sell more, for less. The Supercenter (the combination of food and general merchandise in one enormous box) allowed companies like Wal-Mart to sell a broader range of products for even less money. The creation of the Wholesale Membership Club, typified by concepts like Sam's Club and Costco, created an awesomely efficient way to sell select items in large quantities at unbelievable prices. Dollar stores like Family Dollar and Dollar General focus on imported goods and extremely low cost of operations to achieve their savings. And the European notion of a hard discount store (typified by companies like Aldi) bring together private brands, extremely limited range, and a low-cost store to achieve great savings. The consumer has reaped a windfall of savings, and retailers who have figured out how to sell for less have experienced exponential growth.

While not all innovations in retail have focused on price, it has certainly been a prevalent theme. While exploiting fashion, providing outstanding service, offering an expanded range of products, and selling or manufacturing high-quality merchandise have all shown that available niches exist in all facets of retailing, the notion of bigger and cheaper has been hard to shake. Margins have been reduced in just about every retail business, from food to apparel to electronics. Similar products cost less now after inflation than they did decades before, and consumer buying power has increased. The consumer has had it very good, demanding more for less, and more often than not, getting it.

In our first book, *Winning at Retail*, we extensively documented what amounted to an empirical look at retail success and our theory behind why some retailers win and others lose. We called it the "-Est Theory for Retail Success." The -Est theory derives from the word "best," and essentially says that a retailer must be best—superior to all others—at one core proposition that's important to specific customers. Retailers must strive for this, the notion of owning one key element, rather than attempting to be great at everything for all customers. -Est retailers devote themselves with laser-like focus to their core customer proposition, what we call their "-Est position." They commit employees from top to bottom of their organization to that position. They communicate their -Est position to customers, and execute it relentlessly at the store level. -Est retailers also base strategic and day-to-day operational decisions on their -Est position.

Wal-Mart was cited as the quintessential example of one core -Est element—cheapest. Everything Wal-Mart did for its first 40 years of doing business was focused on enhancing its position as the low-price leader. With its "Always Low Prices," Wal-Mart won with customers. The other -Est positions that win with customers are: Big-Est, having the largest assortment of one merchandise category; Hot-Est, having the right products just as customers begin to buy them in volume; Easy-Est, having service that makes shopping easy; and Quick-Est, having service that makes shopping quick.

We defended the theory by documenting successful retailers' adherence to these basic principles. It took a very rational viewpoint of consumer behavior, suggesting that retailers could be classified into one general area. And hindsight has thankfully proven the theory. But, as with any theory, questions certainly lingered and we engage in many debates, in countless facets of the retail industry, on whether the theory still holds. We are often asked the following:

- Does the notion of an -Est work in every category?
- What about occupying more than one -Est position? Isn't it better to have two or three -Ests rather than one?
- Can an -Est position go away?
- Aren't there multiple facets of an -Est like hot?
- What about quality? Surely there are retailers who win by having the best-performing stuff?
- What about the emotional aspects of connecting with a brand? There seem to be many examples of brands that win not for rational reasons alone but by creating a very real relationship with the customer.

In the very real nuances of positioning a retailer, all of these questions are valid and all need to be accounted for in an increasingly complex and competitive retail world. While we stick to our guns on the need to differentiate and not be everything for everybody, we acknowledge the need for further examination of a retailer's positioning.

It's difficult to argue with the notion of selling products for less. Wal-Mart's mission has long been built under the concept of allowing ordinary people the opportunity to buy more products. It turns out that the execution of this very simple and very pro-consumer positioning strikes at the very core of our social fabric. Manufacturing jobs have all but deserted America as companies have sought to source goods cheaper elsewhere. The deflation of many products has been achieved through cheap global sourcing. What about competitive wages for workers? What about health benefits for employees, as retailing makes up a huge chunk of American jobs? What about protecting smaller retailers without access to the economies of scale of the bigger players? And what about smaller manufacturers (or even bigger ones) who must constantly attempt to take costs out of their products to live up to the relentless cost pressures from retailers? These are all significant issues that the country (and retailers) are dealing with today and challenge the idea that lower prices for consumers is always the best thing for society as a whole.

We have always been proponents of a basic economic stance: "The customer is boss." Or consumers vote with their wallets. One of the inevitable responses that consumers will give in focus groups is nostalgia for the old days. They loved the service at the local hardware store or the intimacy of shopping in town. Well, if consumers liked it so much, how come they switched their spending dollars to Home Depot and away from Bob's Hardware? Again and again, what consumers say and what they do seem to be two very different things.

There is mounting evidence, however, of impending change. Wal-Mart, with its incredible historic growth, has been slowing down of late and has not been able to produce the phenomenal growth that at one point seemed inevitable. Whether it's growing consumer resentment over Wal-Mart's social practices or simply poor execution of retail fundamentals, the retail giant is no longer as successful (or feared) as it once was. While far and away still the largest and most formidable retail organization in the world, its future growth no longer feels as certain. If bigger was better, that surely couldn't happen. Home improvement titan Home Depot is struggling to maintain its customer base and the largest department store chain, Macy's, is also limping along of late.

There is also considerable evidence that the consumer is changing and success can no longer be as easily measured in the simple, rational dimensions of price or having an ample abundance of products. Perhaps big, one-size-fits-all formats are no longer the right formula for success?

And perhaps consumers will begin voting with their values as much as their dollars.

Greentailing and Other Revolutions in Retailing seeks to catalog those changes that are occurring in retail today. They might be revolutions, providing new ways to connect with customers and drive business. This is not a manifesto for going green. We are pragmatic practitioners of the fundamental goal of retail strategy—if it doesn't drive long-term success and profits, don't bother. This is not about feeling good or generating positive public relations but driving sales and profits. We delve into the notion of Greentailing and the implications it's having right now on retailers and suppliers. We look at the key consumer demographic and behavioral changes that are creating the opportunities for new ways to reach consumers. We explore the dynamics of new ways to win with consumers, breaking away from traditional brick-and-mortar, product-driven approaches. And, we tackle the issue of who owns the customer and the changing dynamic between retailer and supplier.

You say you want a revolution? *Greentailing and Other Revolutions in Retailing* may not change the world, but hopefully it will at least encourage people to think about retailing in a whole new way.

INTRODUCTION

What's Going to Revolutionize Retailing in the Future?

The future is already here. It's just unevenly distributed.
— *William Gibson*

William Gibson, the great British science fiction writer, is famous for taking reality as we know it, and with just the slightest shifts, creating a futuristic vision of the world. Although his stories explore an unknown future, they are steeped with enough reality to be plausible. Somewhere, in the hundreds of thousands of existing stores, millions of product on the shelves, and untold dreams in the heads of entrepreneurs, the vision for the future of retailing is already taking shape. It will likely be built on common trends and themes we see today, with that slight "shift" that creates the revolution. As Gibson intimates and we preach, the future is already here, it is just not easy to collect it in one tidy place. We know real change is going to happen; getting there, profitably and fast, is sometimes a very different story.

Every year, hundreds of new concepts and tens of thousands of new products are ambitiously introduced into the marketplace. Very few manage to succeed. Some are bankrolled by multibillion-dollar corporations with reams of data and research. Others are formed on a shoestring budget, operating out of a garage or the trunk of a car. We have been tracking, reviewing, and participating in the development of new concepts for over 20 years at McMillan|Doolittle. We would venture to say we have probably seen more new ideas—realized or scrapped on the drawing board than just about anyone. We trade on this experience to hopefully have a higher batting average of hits versus misses. We are constantly monitoring the retail scene to try to answer some of the fundamental questions:

- Why do some concepts work and others fail?
- Why do some ideas, like the notion of Greentailing suddenly seem to be taking hold after nearly two decades of gestation?
- What other ideas are going to revolutionize the retail landscape?

Most importantly, we often first need to answer the question, who cares? Why is there an obsession with developing new ideas or innovation? If you have a successful concept or product line, what's wrong with running with what you have and making the occasional tweaks along the way? The answer is simple—do you want to be in business 10 years from now?

For a number of reasons, the world of retailing is changing faster and more dramatically than ever before. It is not enough to simply get it right once; winners must continually stay on top of their game or risk an even quicker obsolescence than ever before. With the customer voting daily, the need to stay on top is vital. And there is certainly still an advantage for the retailer or supplier who gets there first. It is always easier to make changes when you're on top than when you're fighting for survival at the back of the pack.

COMPRESSED LIFE CYCLE

It's no secret that retail has been consolidating. There have been more mergers than ever before, consolidating retail power among fewer companies. At the same time, there have been more bankruptcies, with weaker retailers dropping out of the race. Just as importantly, we've also seen the life cycle for stores squeezed. In the past, the retail life cycle looked like a typical bell curve. There's a period of development for an emerging concept, followed by a period of rapid growth, then maturity as the curve flattens, and then eventually there's a decline. That cycle still exists, of course, but it's been significantly compressed as new retail concepts grow, mature, and decline faster than ever:

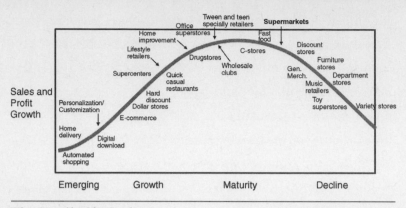

The Retail Life Cycle

Are consumers simply more fickle than before? We don't think so. The abundance of great choice has made them realize that better alternatives do exist. They are simply not as loyal to any store or brand.

The cycle is compressing in part because of the globalization of communications. Ideas can spread almost instantaneously, thanks to the Internet. While good ideas once were able to remain regional and somewhat obscure, that's no longer the case. Ideas and best practices now spread internationally, often in a matter of days, as traditional barriers and borders begin to disappear. When Tesco "secretly" opened its long-awaited entry into the U.S. market called Fresh & Easy, it was a matter of hours before significant intelligence (and lots of opinions) flooded the Internet. Ideas no longer incubate in relative obscurity because they are exposed quickly on an international stage. There is little that is proprietary to a retail concept that has its doors open to the public. They are easy to replicate but hard to run successfully.

The other big squeeze on the life cycle is the high-risk, high-reward influence of venture capital and public markets. Retailers have greater access to funds than they did in the past, both from private and public sources. However, that money comes with strings attached—the expectation of fast growth. As e-commerce showed, the battle for "first-mover" advantage and critical mass has often become the top priority. Getting there first, and with scale, requires a concept to move fast. The result of these activities is a compressed retail life cycle that forces new concepts to come of age quickly. It also puts pressure on older formats and established retailers to innovate, or risk idly sitting by while a fast-moving new concept takes away customers. Staying on top is harder than ever before, and the monthly report card of same-store sales often shows how quickly one's fortune can change. Even before the ink dried on our first book, *Winning at Retail*, some of our "success" examples were beginning to experience hard times.

As proof of the compressing life cycle, we looked at the history of various retail formats. Variety stores like Woolworth and Ben Franklin were the nation's first mass retailers. They are dead now, after about 50 years of existence. Department stores are also about 50 years old and now are clearly in a state of decline, in the process of consolidation rather than rapid growth. Yes, department stores are still important, but discount stores now outsell department stores by about a 4 to 1 ratio, with most of that change occurring in the past 20 years. Discount stores themselves were hatched around 40 years ago. And in just 40 years, they've reached a level of maturity where even the nation's number three discount store, Kmart, is fighting for survival. Meanwhile, the leaders Wal-Mart and Target have both become grocers as a way to continue expanding, and both are trying to figure out new ways to maintain their dominance. The category killer sector, including stores like Home Depot and Toys"R"Us, have been around for 30 years or so. (Note: Toys"R"Us actually was started over 50 years ago, but not in the category killer, large-chain format of today.) These "biggest" type retailers are also mature, and various sectors within this category appear to be in decline. E-commerce retailing, with all its hype and irrational exuberance, matured in less than a decade to the point where many start-ups were forced out of business and growth rates will soon be approaching 10 percent to 15 percent annually rather than the 50 percent to 100 percent growth of the past.

Life cycles are shrinking so dramatically that it's nearly gotten to the point where investors, retailers, and retail suppliers should begin to think about stores the same way investors think about dance clubs or trendy restaurants. Those types of businesses are notorious for being big money-makers for two or three years, then either limping along for a time or simply going away. The investment strategy is to get in fast, make lots of money, then get out. While retail may never move quite as fast as hip restaurants and night clubs, the lesson is plain: In today's market, stores must be able to adapt to new market conditions very quickly. Successful companies then need to be judged not only on their ability to get it right once, but also on their ability to innovate and change as consumers and competition dictates. And they must be able to do so in a high-pressure environment, where separating out the fads from long-term trends is extremely difficult. Getting out may be just as important as getting in—there have been several notable plugs pulled of late (The Gap's Forth & Towne or Finish Line's Paiva) where the trend was there but the companies themselves were not able to capitalize on it.

The trick, then, is to maintain a solid position on the growth side of a retail life cycle. This may mean developing a new format to participate in a growing market or radically revamping an existing one to maintain relevancy. In a world where it is increasingly difficult to find a one-size-fits-all format, it might mean doing all of the above—looking for a new concept for growth while retooling an existing one.

What are the common ways that retailers lose their way? We have identified four classic patterns:

1. *Innovative new competition:* Competition truly has to be accounted for on a local level. Customers shop the stores in their trade areas. A retailer simply has to be the best in its marketplace to succeed. In the absence of better competition, a retailer can succeed in its market, temporarily. But, eventually, a better competitor will come along and supplant that retailer's existing position. That retailer can come from the next town, region of the country, or increasingly, from another part of the world. Even more daunting, he or she may come to market in the form of an e-commerce competitor, or a

direct seller, or other form that radically changes the rules of the game.

2. *Stakes are raised:* Sometimes, a new competitor enters the market and changes the very nature of competition, raising the standards of how customers view your stores. A company may have indeed achieved a sustainable difference, only to see a new competitor change the standard. -Est levels (what it takes to be the best) have been rising—and what it takes to maintain an -Est position is tougher than ever before. Your competitor may not even operate the same format—consumers are constantly exposed to formats from all kinds of retailers and their expectations of what is an acceptable experience are often influenced by such changes. If a home improvement retailer innovates with a new format, it could have implications on how customers view shopping for shoes or a new car.

3. *Eye off the ball:* And, of course, there are companies that fall out of -Est in an entirely self-inflicted manner. They simply lose track of what their customers are looking for in a shopping experience. They fail to read their own data, consumer research, or pay close enough attention to what their competitors are doing. Companies like Toys"R"Us and Home Depot, we would argue, lost track of what was important to their customers, allowing competition to enter their markets.

4. *Customer change:* While it is easy to look back and see the enormity of demographic shifts, they are sometimes

hard to see when they are happening. Customers do change—their profile, attitudes and beliefs, and patterns. As retailers, we typically respond later than we should to these consumer shifts.

The end result of all this pressure from competitors, customers, and investors is a vice-like squeeze on the market like retailers have never experienced before. When you also consider the trend that many people want to spend less time shopping, the implication is clear. Pretty good isn't good enough any more. Consumers don't want more stores; and they don't want more retail square footage. They want better retailers.

As we begin to look at *Greentailing and other Revolutions in Retail*, we need to do so with the mindset that what might begin as a small kernel could one day blossom into an all-out trend. While Greentailing is attracting a huge amount of publicity and an emerging band of entrepreneurial suppliers and retailers, we would be the first to admit that it doesn't mean big business today. A simple reaction to Greentailing would be to follow one of two relatively obvious paths: ignore it and hope it goes away or pay it nominal lip service. Both allow retailers to go about their business in the same manner as before, with minimal disruption and certainly a minimal impact on sales. While this attitude might serve to maximize the shortterm, it does have some flaws:

- When major change does happen, it comes fast. As we discuss in the next chapter on inflection points, change doesn't happen on a simple curve.

- If you fall behind, the chances of catching up are very, very difficult. The consumer and competition is unforgiving.

Greentailing is a crucial element of the future of retail. Perhaps it is the key to understanding a seismic shift in consumer behavior that shifts the balance away from price to other factors that will require businesses to rethink their basic models. Perhaps it will require a complete retooling of the way business is conducted—a change in the attitude of cheaper-at-all-costs to a formula far more complex. We expect that a new future for retailing will emerge. Our goal is to provide you with provocative, interesting, and potentially valuable insights into that future. We hope to follow Gibson's lead and make it a bit easier to manage.

CHAPTER ONE

INFLECTION POINTS IN RETAILING

A strategic inflection point is a time in the life of a business when its fundamentals are about to change. They are the result of an event which changes the way we think or act.

—*Andrew S. Grove, ex-Chairman, Intel*

We speculate that the success or failure of retail companies is not the result of short-term actions but rather the culmination of a series of decisions made over time. Successful companies consistently and accurately anticipate or create new market trends. Those less successful either fail to react to market conditions or simply make the wrong choices. The companies have lagging sales and profits over a long period of time—then suddenly make headlines as the financial consequences of their actions come to bear. They become candidates for our ever-growing list of companies who have entered the Black Hole of Retail—where companies head in but rarely make it out.

The concept of an *inflection point* suggests that there are critical points in the history of an industry or an individual company that signal permanent and enduring change. When a company faces an inflection point, its future might literally be at stake—the proper responses to these signs lead to sustained growth, while inappropriate reactions often lead to obsolescence.

It is easy to reflect back on the past and point out retrospectively where these right or wrong decisions were made. It is more difficult, but also more informative, for retailers and suppliers to recognize if an impending inflection point is at hand. And even more critically, to have the necessary skill sets to predict those potential inflection points and respond quickly and appropriately. Knowing when to react to a trend versus ignoring a fad, and doing it again and again, helps certain companies stay relevant, efficient, and ultimately successful.

Andy Grove, the founder and ex-chairman of Intel is credited with popularizing the concept of an inflection point and bringing the term into popular usage in the business world. While the term is often used (and perhaps overused) in the modern business lexicon, what about its applicability to retailing? What really signifies an inflection point as it relates to the retail business? We postulate as follows:

> An inflection point is a formative occurrence—a permanent shift in the competitive situation that forever changes the way business is done.

In plainer English—miss a big inflection point and you could be in big trouble. What makes it difficult is determining where the inflection point occurs. Rather, a series of conditions appear to exist in the market that leads to a retailer response and the subsequent creation of an inflection point. It is hardly just one thing and hardly ever packaged together in a neat and tidy way. There are plenty of tea leaves that need to be read.

The concepts of *accelerators* and *disruptors* have been introduced to describe the notion of disruptive change in the marketplace. Retail is in a steady state of evolution, with literally thousands of decisions and changes made on a daily basis. Inflection points represent those moments in time that upset the status quo and represent a significant and permanent shift in the market. Those changes are often the result of companies' responses to accelerators and disruptors.

For example, consumer changes (e.g., aging demographics, smaller household sizes, increasing ethnicity) are often cited as accelerators that invite retailer responses. It is those retailer responses that define the actual inflection point. Similarly, the introduction of a new competitor or format represents a disruptor to the market, either due to the impact of that format itself or the competitive response to that retailer's entry.

INFLECTION POINT MODEL

The inflection point model is illustrated in Figure 1.1. The market moves at a steady rate of change until a significant response is made to accelerators or disruptors occurring in the market.

Some retailers respond innovatively and appropriately, gaining share; others either fail to react or have the wrong response and suffer reduced sales and share.

Create or React

In simple terms, retailers have two options in responding to accelerators or disruptors in the marketplace:

1. They can consciously choose to create their own futures, in effect, creating their own inflection points.

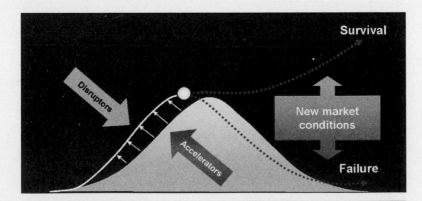

Figure 1.1   Inflection Point Created in Response to Distributors and Accelerators

These retailers are leading change, creating an inflection point based on their own responses to market conditions. While it seems like a retailer would always want to be on the leading edge, there are times when getting out too far ahead can result in considerable losses.

2. Or, they can choose to respond to the changes in the marketplace created by another company. It is often the reaction to change (not the initial change itself) that has the greatest impact on defining the inflection point. While we don't recommend lagging too far behind, it is often not a bad idea to let others lead the charge, then quickly imitate.

Depending on the size, niche, resources, and skills of a particular retailer, either response might be appropriate. The key is being in a position to quickly evaluate the market situation and develop the appropriate response for the organization. One of our business mantras is *Moving Doesn't Always Guarantee Success but Standing Still Is a Sure Way to Lose.* The marketplace is simply too demanding not to change.

As we look at the emergence of Greentailing, it is clear that a number of disruptive factors are now at play. As we detail in later chapters, the classic factors for an inflection point occurrence are all very much in evidence. Whether your company embraces the tenants of Greentailing, one thing is certain—an intelligent, strategic response is needed. It is a trend that cannot be ignored. Your customers, competitors, and the media are making certain of that.

What's Involved in Getting It Right?

Simply spotting a trend isn't enough. Developing an appropriate and timely response and having an organization capable of achieving dramatic change are also enormous challenges.

The ultimate manifestation of a response to change in the market is the creation of a new format, or the radical reconstitution of an existing one. While retailers make hundreds or thousands of iterative changes on a daily or weekly basis, true change comes along rarely. And revolutionary change even more rarely than that.

One of the reasons that format creation is such a challenge is that it's hard to get right. A new format must correctly find the intersection of consumer change, competitive differentiation, and be powered by the internal competencies to succeed. And, by the way, it would be nice if it made some money as well. Getting it right is truly an art form.

There is no more animated discussion within our consulting business than when it comes to rendering an opinion on a new retail concept or a major new idea within a store. It is the retail consultant equivalency of a really great bar argument. A new concept or prototype is the culmination of divine inspiration, blood, sweat, and tears and countless hours of strategizing and research. For anyone involved in a retail industry, opening a new concept is one of the most exciting events. It is also one of the most difficult things to get right, and you can crunch numbers and study it to death, but it is almost impossible to actually determine how a consumer will interact once they're in a newly created retail environment.

We've been chronicling change in retailing for almost 20 years as part of our *Retail Watch* newsletter. We started *Retail Watch* to provide an editorialized view on new ideas after getting tired of reading hyped-up press releases or glowing articles that never mentioned any flaws. We've logged millions of miles traversing the globe to see new ideas only to be disappointed to see a store that clearly wasn't cutting it with the ultimate judge, the customer. Our favorite example of this is "store of the year" design awards, which almost guarantee a concept's doom. (Remember, customers don't buy store designs.) So, we have taken a point of view, in a slightly irreverent way to actually criticize the formats we visit. Our criteria is pretty simple—we have to experience a store to write about it and we have to visit anonymously. By the way, you can add "guided tours" with the retailer's management among our other pet peeves—we want to see stores as customers see them—not when they've been prettied up for the royal tour.

As part of studying new retail concepts or formats, we always ask ourselves: Have we seen "the future of retailing?" which we once proclaimed after visiting the prototype Wal-Mart Supercenter way back in 1990, or have we seen something that will likely be written off the books in short order? Or worse yet, will the failure to create a new format that profitably connects with the customer cement a company's path to retail oblivion, which we affectionately call the Black Hole?

If so much is riding on the success of creating a new concept, how do you actually go about creating one? What are the rules and lessons that might apply that will help retailers avoid some of the costly mistakes and lead to a better chance of success? It is our fundamental belief that much can be learned about future success by studying what's currently working and extrapolating those lessons into something new and exciting.

How Do You Know if You're on the Right Path?

With all of the new retail formats opening these days, there are a number of arguments about what's working, not working, and most importantly, why? Why does one concept become a breakthrough while others simply break down? We have been involved in development of a number of retail formats that have succeeded and some that have failed and, because we have reviewed every significant new concept to come along in retailing over the past 20 years, we have a right to a few strong points of view:

- *No one, ever, has nailed a new concept, right off the bat.* In fact, the "newer," the tougher it is to pull off. There are so many moving parts and pieces that it is nearly impossible to get them all in sync. So, we need to look for glimmers of what a finished concept might be like, not the total picture in front of us.

- *There are no overnight successes.* Name a concept, any concept, and you will typically find a rather lengthy pattern of development and evolution until someone gets it right. The key to profitable retailing is replication—once you get beyond prototype, the real money lies in rolling out a formula.

- *It is absolutely critical to get the customer and the experience right.* That's where it gets tricky and where the real debate should lie in understanding a concept. Is it right on consumer trend? Does it have the right products? Mix? Design? Experience? Pricing? And so on. We would argue that nailing the customer and the experience is most critical—the others will follow—assuming you have the time and resources. But, you better have the right products and services to sell—customers don't buy a store design.

- *Make sure it is sustainable.* There have been many concepts that look great out of the gate, only to falter later. Think Krispy Kreme. Distinguishing between a faddish concept, versus ones that can stand the test of time, is sometimes tough to do. Ensuring that a concept has sustainability, defined by repeat customer visits, is critical.

It is fairly easy to look at new retail concepts (and we will be looking at a number of new ones in this book) and find fault with almost all of them. The real trick—finding the roots of a concept that can be grown and nourished versus the ones that might wither away because there are fatal flaws (consumer, financial, or whatever).

As to the current state of "green," there is an emergent crop of retail formats, retail departments, and new items that are competing for elusive success. Because we are early in the game, there are few ideas we have seen that truly qualify as unbridled successes. The consumer's intent versus actual actions still seems to be misaligned—saying you are "green" and truly purchasing "green" seem to be quite different at this moment. Green products have historically had a perceptual stigma of lower quality or effectiveness (some of it deserved) at higher prices. And helping the customer understand all of the complexities of green is not an easy task.

The road to revolution in retailing is always a bumpy one. There are plenty of pioneers who are out there, often with arrows in their backs, the consequence of getting too far ahead of the consumer, supply chain, or sustainable business model. There are also the trailers, who simply never catch up. In this book, we examine, in detail, some of the hot ideas that are going to revolutionize retailing. We provide a road map on how to profitably respond for the long term.

New inflection points are at hand, and retailing will never be the same. The bandwagon has arrived, and revolution is on its way.

CHAPTER TWO

TRENDS ARE INTER-CONNECTED

It is not the strongest species that survive, not the most intelligent, but the ones most responsive to change.[1]

—*Charles Darwin*

Strategic planning has been defined as *the management of change, with the intelligent adaptation of external circumstances leading to a conscious creation of a desired future.* A mouthful, to be sure, but one that is a perfect expression of what companies must do to thrive in the marketplace now and in the future. As Darwin said, you don't have to be the biggest or smartest, just the best at recognizing change and actually having the mechanisms in place to effectively respond. Task one, then, is to identify those "external circumstances" that are going to require a response.

START WITH THE CUSTOMER, PLEASE!

If there is one constant in retailing, it is that long-term trends usually stem from consumer-driven changes. And while fads may come and go (in many cases, thankfully), real change is typically accompanied by significant and permanent changes with the customer. Demographics, generational values, and life stages are powerful influencers of behavioral change, and retailers need to pay close attention and respond appropriately. And often they do, generally making minor adjustments in their tactics. In fact, retailers make thousands of changes on almost a continual basis. They must decide what to buy, how much to buy, how much to price items, how to display and sell them, and so on. The business is so driven by the constant need to make quick decisions that it can be a bit overwhelming and certainly extremely time consuming.

Because there are so many details involved in getting the day-to-day operations right, there is seemingly little time left for retailers to reflect on the sea of changes that might be occurring around them. Rarely do retailers make major adjustments in strategy or respond in a significant way, which is why most trends evolve slowly.

Nevertheless, major trend-shifting events do occur in the marketplace. During these critical periods of trend shifting or turning points, markets fundamentally change. Retailers who recognize these signals and formulate a response prosper. Those who don't, struggle to survive or simply disappear. Most frustrating, they are often left without being able to articulate why their customers began leaving them in the first place. In the most ironic twist, the moment to be most concerned about the future may be exactly when profitability is at its highest. Things seem to be fine, and complacency has a way of creeping in. It is at that point that customers are just about to leave you. And, most customers never complain—they simply walk away.

Projecting where retail is headed is a challenging task— as difficult as predicting the next major turn in the business cycle. We do know, however, that the companies who have correctly navigated major changes are the ones who are winning today, and the ones who seem to have developed that sixth sense to change when the time is right. If you don't like our fancy definition of strategic planning, we can substitute a far simpler and usually more memorable one. When Wayne Gretzky, perhaps the greatest ice hockey player ever, was asked by a reporter how he seemed to play a different game than everyone else, he responded:

"I skate to where the puck is going to go."[2]

The answer was simple for an intuitively great player who wasn't the biggest, fastest, or strongest player on the ice—don't simply follow the puck, show up where it's headed. There's no question that Darwin would have been a Gretzky fan.

In the case of retailing, "where the puck is headed" seems to be at the intersection of correctly anticipating the consumer and meeting their needs at precisely the right time.

POWER OF DEMOGRAPHICS

Demographics are powerful predictors of consumer behavior. They shape when, what, how, why, and where consumers shop. Several macrodemographic trends have been driving consumer behavior for the past 25 years and will likely continue for another 25 years. It turns out that demographic trends are clearly predictable trends because they are based on some pretty powerful and often immutable forces. They are frequently talked about by retailers but rarely seem to be acted on. They bear mentioning here to establish a foundation of what will become the driver of future retail revolutions, they also will help us shed some light on the issue of why green and why now.

These well-recognized and important demographic trends include:

* *Aging population:* In 1980, 56 million people in the United States (25 percent of the population) were over 50 years old. Today, 90 million people are over the age of 50. In five years, most of these same people will be over the age of 55. One thing we know about people as they age: They become extremely demanding. They've purchased most everything several times in their lives; they know what they want and what they don't. A tough group to please. We also know that creating stereotypes around "old" people is also a danger. The expectations and lifestyles of today's 50-, 60-, or 70-year-old is very different than what it was a generation or so ago. While

we have yet to see a successful "old person's store," it does not mean that there are not a huge variety of needs that must be addressed and a gold mine for retailers who better cater to this significant demographic. As part of this aging process, retailers often don't know who their customers really are. When we ask our retail clients the average age of their customers, they almost always miss it by eight or more years on the low side (i.e., they think their customers are younger than they really are).

- *Changing households:* Today, 75 percent of eligible adult women are in the workforce, and single heads of households now outnumber married households. Most women don't have enough time for traditional activities and chores, including shopping. Add to this the growing number of smaller, fragmented households, and retailers are left with a clear challenge: rethink formats, products, and services to better meet the needs of working women as well as nontraditional households. Again, it sounds simple but too many retail stores are still built with a traditional nuclear family in mind. Missing out on who your customer really is tends to be a cardinal sin among many retailers who are seemingly stuck in a time warp of who their customers are versus who they idealize them to be.

- *Exploding ethnicity:* In 1980, 20 percent of the U.S. population belonged to four key ethnic groups: Black, Hispanic, Asian, and American Indian. In 2007, that number was approaching 32 percent and "ethnic" populations are continuing to grow at a far greater pace than the White marketplace. Hispanics represent the largest portion (roughly half), and are the fastest growing segment of the population. But, with any stereotype, generalizations are extremely dangerous. The Asian population is extremely fragmented and split into multiple ethnicities. The Hispanic consumer with Mexican origins is different from those of Cuban or Puerto Rican descent. The degree of ethnicity varies significantly by neighborhood, city, and state. But, make no mistake, catering to diverse population needs are a given—the state of Texas is made up of over half ethnic populations and so are many of the major cities in the United States.

- *Polarization of income:* The disparity in buying power between the "haves" and "have-nots" has increased significantly over the past 25 years. Real growth in household income in the United States over this period has been concentrated in the top quintile of households, with most of that increase going to the top 5 percent. The rest of U.S. society is living on practically the same budget they faced some 25 years ago. As a result, the majority of U.S. consumers seek products that provide equal or better quality at a lower price. Retail sales have generally experienced the same type of have and have-not bracketing. Discount stores have far outpaced the sales of department stores. Concepts aimed at the very top quintile have flourished as have those aimed at a lower demographic. Retailers have definitely wanted to be anywhere but the shrinking middle.

CONSUMER BEHAVIOR CHANGES
AND DEMOGRAPHY

Demographics and life stage shifts are major contributors to behavioral change. Societal factors and generational values also play a key role. Most of these changes are having a significant impact on retailers. Many of these changes will linger, become more important, or mutate into new trends in the future. The big five trends in consumer behavior impacting retailing today include:

1. *Market polarization:* Consumer preference for premium offerings on one hand and no-frills offerings on the other are squeezing out middle-of-the-road products and services. Who we think of as the "average" middle class consumer is disappearing. Mass luxury items have become affordable, and shoppers "trade up" on items in which quality/prestige is key. They also "trade down" where saving money is more important. Increasingly, the same consumer trades up and trades down during the same trip to the same retailer or shopping center. Target ingeniously positions itself to serve both needs by telling customers to "Expect More, Pay Less." And typical generalization of consumers no longer works—the same customer may go to Aldi and Coach on the same shopping trip—for very different reasons.

2. *Time compression:* Many Americans feel their life is a race against the clock. It's more than just a lack of time; it's the challenge of managing time in small segments.

Convenience, simplification, and finding complete solutions are priorities, as is utilizing the Internet to balance time demands. Retailers need to rethink their offer to determine how to provide more convenience to their customers. But, convenience will take on an expanded definition to include offering ways to more intelligently customize assortments, utilizing multichannel shopping strategies, employing intelligent technology to improve all facets of the shopping experience, and, of course, rethinking store sizes and formats. Consumers place a tangible value on their time as well as their dollars—both are precious commodities.

3. *Control:* Consumers, especially baby boomers, want to be in control of their lives and shopping experiences, and the Internet has opened the door for them to establish more control in retail and direct shopping. Consumers can obtain complete knowledge about virtually any product and service and compare and contrast their options online. They have more choices over where they shop, when they shop, and even what they will pay for an item. Consumer advocacy, customer reviews and ratings, and actual customer experiences in the store and online are perceived as more credible than traditional forms of communication and are actually reshaping retail advertising and marketing. The balance of power has shifted away from the retailer (or brand) controlling the experience to the consumer having a greater and more influential role.

Retailers who make it easy for the customer to gain control of the experience, and who have transparency in their business operations will thrive.

4. *Shifting preferences:* Today's most compelling products and services facilitate experiences that deliver much more than just function. Retailers and suppliers traditionally sold products—today's customers are looking for solutions and experiences within those products. Across retailing, consumer preferences are shifting from buying goods to buying goods and services, from purchasing mass produced products to looking for individualization and customization, from acquiring single items to finding complete solutions, and from consuming a product to establishing a lifelong experience. The concept of lifestyle retailing speaks to a different way of thinking about what function a retailer really serves. The farther up the experience pyramid a retailer can ascend, the less important role price plays in the equation.

5. *Wellness:* Society at large has an increased focus on the pursuit of wellness. Attention to weight loss, anti-aging, vitality, and beauty is growing as people are getting older, living longer, and looking for ways to enhance their lives. This pertains to all aspects of consumers' lives from what they eat to what they put on and in their bodies. Serving the many facets of the wellness equation, from prevention to health-care needs offers a tremendous opportunity for retailers

and service providers. As the population ages and demand increases, we expect to see a multitude of new products and formats designed to meet the wellness needs of consumers.

DISRUPTERS AND ACCELERANTS

Strategic inflection points are normally caused by an external disrupter or accelerant that forces change to the status quo. Ongoing trends that everyone is anchored to, suddenly shift direction. In other words, a catalyst appears that takes small trends and turns them into a large one. Developing insights into what causes these significant shifts is critical to successfully preparing for the changes that follow.

There are a number of prime candidates today that are potential accelerants or disruptors to the retail marketplace:

- *Technology:* The speed of adoption of new technology today is phenomenal. As a result, technology has become the most significant accelerator (and disrupter) of change over the past 10 years. Young shoppers expect technology in the retail environment while older shoppers may not tolerate it. One size does not currently fit all with technology, and retailers must straddle two generations—an older generation that sees technology as functional and sometimes unnecessary and a younger generation that has grown up with play, learning, and entertainment intertwined in technology. And clearly Internet technology has changed the way people shop.

By 2010, it will influence nearly one-half of total U.S. retail sales and e-commerce will continue to grow in direct sales faster than traditional retail. The trouble with technology is that it can have a very long incubation period followed by sudden adoption. It is easy at times to follow the slow pace of technology adoption and conclude that nothing really will have an impact. Examples of latent retail technology in recent years include electronic shelf tags, digital signage solutions, electronic shopping cart technology, pay-by-touch systems, self-payment technologies, and electronic kiosks to name a few. All have been introduced in various times with great fanfare but few seem to have a big initial impact. But when they do hit, watch out—they can have a major impact on the business. Others to watch include Radio Frequency Identification (RFID), mobile payment solutions, and self-scanning technologies to eliminate the need for front ends. A common mistake too many retailers make is looking at technology for technology's sake as opposed to first understanding the consumer issue that it is trying to solve.

- *Innovation:* Innovation in retail comes in cycles. After a slow period in the 1990s (other than Internet technology), we are beginning to see new and innovative ideas in brick-and-mortar retailing. In fact, we believe the single factor contributing most to the accelerating pace of change in the retail business environment will be innovation. New formats, new experiences, and new services will be required as part of the next innovations cycle in retailing. Given today's shortening retail life cycle, the failure to innovate will lead to rapid obsolescence.

- *Geopolitical events:* Every society faces potential unknown threats that radically alter consumer behavior and disrupt existing trends. The speed of information penalizes a retailer who has a delayed reaction. Proactive preparedness for these eventualities is the defense against potential negative ramifications. Examples of recent unknown threats are terrorism and natural disasters. Global warming may be a candidate for the future. The lack of water in developing nations could have major ramifications on the global economy. The threat of pandemics is very real and could have an impact on the supply chain as evidenced by a spate of recent product safety issues, from ground beef to toys to pet food. One of these potential trend shifts could in fact lead to a much faster adoption of a latent trend.

- *Societal change:* Consumer attitudes are constantly changing and dramatic shifts can accelerate or disrupt current trends. Attitudes and changes that we are currently tracking include: corporate accountability, environmental concerns, consumer demand for authenticity, and self-invention or self-actualization (as a spin-off from wellness). As society mutates, so must retailers. It is entirely possible that these "softer" trends will have as big an impact as the "hard" demographic or economic trends that are usually given so much focus and attention.

- *Economic bubbles:* A number of economic bubbles exist in the United States (and the world) today. If deflated rapidly, they could significantly impact the economy and consumer expenditures (the key driver of retail sales). If just one of these economic bubbles burst, the impact would be felt in some sectors, but would not likely have significant impact across all retailing. However, many of these economic bubbles are interrelated, and multiple economic bubble bursts would clearly result in a tipping point across all retailing segments. For far too long, retailers have counted on the consumer to simply defy economic gravity—spend no matter what.

Our list of economic bubbles at risk a year ago also included an overhyped stock market and overvalued real estate, but these bubbles have popped, and retailers suffered, especially among retailers directly related to the home. As the current economic and political crises play themselves out, it is clear that retailing, as an integral part of society and the economy, is inextricably linked to both.

Not all accelerants or disruptors can be predicted or planned for, but successful retailers study and monitor them on an ongoing basis. Good retailers have contingency plans to deal with these special situations as they arise.

PUTTING IT ALL TOGETHER

Putting it all together, the picture in Figure 2.1 emerges.

Demographics are huge drivers themselves and also spawn significant behavioral changes in consumers. Those changes are provoked by catalysts, those accelerators and

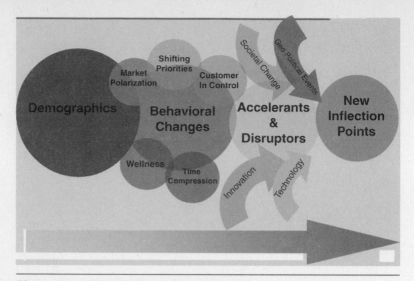

Figure 2.1   Trends Are Interconnected

disruptors that lead to the development of an inflection point. This theory seems to make sense, but how does it manifest itself in practice.

If Greentailing is in fact a long-term sustainable trend, we should be able to match consumer shifts and our understanding of inflection points against this emerging trend. How will these trends come together to fuel the Greentailing Revolution?

Greentailing seems to be hitting at the rare intersection of overlapping demography with fuel from social and political trends. Green appeals to the aging baby boomer, who is belatedly waking up to generations of waste. Go to any grade school, on the other extreme, and you will find young children being raised to be more environmentally responsible. Behavior-wise, green seems inextricably linked with many of the principles of wellness and a shift in priorities away from materialism. Throw political and media pressure into the pot as powerful stimulants and the results are what we see today—a lot of noise on green. The big question, to paraphrase Shakespeare: Is this sound and fury we are hearing today signifying nothing or is there substance underneath?

CHAPTER THREE

GREENTAILING 2.0—THE SECOND GENERATION OF GREEN

Earth-friendly products won't save the Earth if they don't save people money.[1]

—*Wal-Mart Advertisement*

From Wal-Mart's pragmatic ad copy to Barneys' 2007 "Have a Green Holiday" catalog featuring a $1,000 plus recyclable canvas bag, two things are very clear about Greentailing circa 2008:

1. It is the cause du jour among many retailers, even those with significantly different missions.
2. There are wildly different interpretations about what "green" really means when it pertains to retail.

The *New York Times* article, "A World Consumed by Guilt," nicely lays out both the sentiment of consumers to be more sensible in their purchasing and the extreme difficulties of interpreting what being green necessarily entails. Paula Schwartz writes,

---

"No matter how sincere fashion designers may be in their efforts to embrace the green movement this season, consumers may find themselves perplexed by how to gauge the environmental impact of the many products that claim to be eco-friendly."[2]

For all types of retailers, there is a challenge in conveying green initiatives in a clear way for consumers to understand them. This book clarifies what Greentailing really means, evaluates what the consumer is saying and why it is important, examines how different retailers are interpreting green, and provides some practical tips to bring businesses further along on this seminal topic.

Right up front, we tackle a fundamental paradox regarding the intersection of retailing and the world of green: If retailers really want to take steps to preserve the environment, all they need to do is to get consumers to spend less and consume less. Simple, really. Loblaw's, the largest retailer in Canada, currently has its stores plastered with the message "Spend Less." We assume they are referring to the fact that they have lower prices. But in retailing, you need to be very careful about what you wish for. We don't really want our customers to spend less (though Loblaw's current earnings shortfalls do indicate that they are succeeding in their unintended goal).

Spending and consuming less is a premise that goes against the grain of the goal of consumerism, which is to get consumers to spend more and consume more. We continually entice them with better products, new must-have styles and technologies, fantastic customer service and aspirational marketing, all with the explicit goal of having them spend more. And yes, ironically, offering lower prices is a tried-and-true way to get registers to ring.

With a patriotic spin, spending more is not just important for the stock prices of retailers and suppliers, it is critical for our economic prosperity—we are driven by the notion of consumerism. It is little wonder, then, that this issue of Greentailing is an extraordinarily difficult one for retailers and suppliers to tackle on a number of levels. And it leads to the potential paradox:

How do we present the appearance of being green while still making sure that we meet our business goals?

Thus, we are presented with two unique interpretations of green. Wal-Mart's interpretation of environmentalism that suggests that being green really only makes sense if the customers themselves save money. No social agenda here—just what it does for you personally? Or Barneys' mea culpa of "go ahead and spend all you want. A portion of what you spend goes to good causes." Trickle-down environmentalism, indeed.

To be clear, we make our living at McMillan|Doolittle helping retailers make more money by effectively selling more stuff and selling more stuff profitably. It is no accident that the subtitle of this book is "Hot Ideas That Are Grabbing Customers' Attention and Raising Profits." We take a very pragmatic approach to the issue of green by reverting back to asking the simple question: What do our customers want us to do now and in the very near future? And how do we do it in a way that ensures retailers can continue to grow revenues and profits? It certainly appears, as we lay out in subsequent chapters, that consumers are looking for retailers and suppliers to act more responsibly, and consumers may even be prepared to pay more or switch their allegiances to companies that embrace green. If that's the case, then Greentailing must be approached, at a minimum, with a pragmatic view toward protecting market share and profits. We also believe that it can become the platform for a fundamental shift in business practices. Yes, green (environmentalism) might really mean green (profits).

We call this chapter "Greentailing 2.0" for two reasons: 1.) Green has been around a long time and can hardly be considered a new movement. We can trace back the origins of green nearly 40 years and remember similar moments in the past where green appeared to be poised to become much more significant. 2.) By the time this book is published, we will have been bombarded by the early waves of green. Hardly a day goes by when there isn't a new research study or a new response to the growing importance of

> Greentailing 2.0 is conscientious retailing built on environmentally sustainable, socially responsible, and economically profitable business practices which explicitly consider the impact of a retailer's actions on the environment and community, customer perception and behavior, employees, suppliers, and ultimately shareholder returns.

environmentalism. We are seeking to move beyond the hype and focus on what is concrete in this area.

GREENTAILING 2.0 DEFINED

We define Greentailing 2.0 as follows:

In creating this definition, we consciously chose to take the broadest definition of what green can encompass. This includes not only the narrow definition of "saving the environment" but places "conscience retailing" at the forefront of all business activities.

Greentailers actively seek to sell products and services while minimizing the impact on the environment and to adopt operating practices that minimize waste. This is more than simply carrying "green" products—it often involves substantial supply chain work to meet green standards and ensure that green products can be competitive on the shelf. Progressive Greentailers are leading the charge in proactively changing their business practices to be more responsible global citizens. They are not simply waiting for new legislation to tell them what they must do. Retailing has long been defined by its passive approach to issues around consumerism—let the government determine standards and we'll follow them. While this worked in the past, it is unlikely to hold water in the future.

If it all sounds a bit preachy, it may well be. One significant reason for this is the ability to define substance against hype. Consumers today have access to significantly more information than they did in the past, and the viral nature of communications makes it far too easy to expose practices that are more for show than substance. If suppliers and retailers believe that they can manage green through a public relations campaign, they are likely to experience real consumer backlash.

BEWARE OF GREENWASHING

Retailers must be cautious of the pitfalls of *greenwashing*. Greenwashing is the act of misleading consumers about an organization's environmentally friendly practices, products, or services. However, consumers are savvy enough to catch on, especially if the messaging is inconsistent with the overall experience. Watchdog groups monitor the sincerity in green messaging. Enviromedia, a Web-based watchdog group, created a Greenwashing Index in January 2008 that uses user-submitted ads and assesses companies' green messages against their green actions. The interactive forum allows users to rate the ads based on greenwashing criteria with a score of 5 equaling "total greenwashing" and a score of 1 equaling a "good ad" (see Table 3.1).

Table 3.1   Greenwashing Index Sampling of Ads

Company	Advertisement	Rating (1–5)
Chevron	Untapped energy commercial	1.6
BP	Global climate change commercial	1.85
Enterprise Rent-A-Car	Blue skies commercial	2.3
Volkswagen	Carbon neutral project print ad	3.15
Ford	Kermit the frog commercial for Ford Escape	4.36
Chevrolet	E85 commercial	4.45

1 = Good ad; 3 = Pushing it; 5 = Total greenwashing.

Source: The Enviromedia Greenwashing Index web site, http://www.greenwashingindex.com (accessed January 17, 2008).

Retailers and suppliers alike must answer a fundamental question—are we committed to practicing what we preach or are we implementing green initiatives to "check the box" of things we feel we must do to be competitive in the future? There are many examples of greenwashing where the well-intended efforts of the larger retail organization don't match the reality on the sales floor. Greentailing requires an integrated effort on the part of the whole organization and a fundamental belief that it is the right thing to do.

Complicating these efforts is the lack of a uniform understanding as to what constitutes Greentailing and the difficulty of navigating the trade-offs involved in doing green well. There are no easy answers. The goal then, is a commitment by retailers and suppliers to act ethically in an economically, socially, and environmentally sustainable manner. The rise of ethical consumerism has brought green center stage, and retailers are changing their practices to meet consumer demand and stay ahead of the game. Many retailers and suppliers have demonstrated that green practices aren't prohibitively costly and can actually represent a cost savings in both the short and long term. And, in a number of instances, solutions can be created that in fact benefit retailers, suppliers, and the consumer alike. A combination of green credibility and well-run green operations has proven to be a successful model for Greentailers.

THE GREEN MOVEMENT

The idea of "green" has been with us for quite some time. April 22, 1970, marked the first Earth Day celebrated in the United States. Through legislative action, a day was designated as a platform for discussion and demonstration for green events and issues. Americans came together with concern over the deterioration of the environment and the consumption of resources, demonstrating that they cared and that they were ready for stronger political action.

This event may have marked the official beginning of environmentalism and resource sustainability as a part of consumer consciousness here in the United States, though numerous grassroots movements occurred during the activist days of the late 1960s. Earth Day began the dialogue and brought to the mainstream issues like ozone depletion, climate change, resource depletion, toxic air, water pollution, and waste management.

Why is green such a big deal now? While the movement has made somewhat steady progress, the commercial impact has been remarkably slow over a period of 30-plus years. As one example, we can trace the growth in more responsible reporting on behalf of some of the largest companies.

In 2005, 68 percent of the world's 250 largest corporations issued reports on their environmental performance, compared with 50 percent in 2002 and 35 percent in 1999.[3]

Today, corporate responsibility reporting has hit the mainstream and is standard practice among corporations. In fact, corporations have created positions dedicated to managing their green efforts, with titles like corporate responsibility officer.

For all of the talk, green-influenced retail has been an extremely small piece of the economy until quite recently. What's changed? It seems that Greentailing represents an inflection point on the cusp (a seminal moment in time when a market changes forever). It exhibits all of the classic trademarks, a long period of somewhat steady movement that is acted on by a series of accelerators or disruptors that drive rapid change. What are those disruptors? While there is no singular definition, the common factors are as follows:

- *External factors:* The film, *An Inconvenient Truth,* which premiered in the spring of 2006, featured former Vice President Al Gore orating about scientific opinion on climate change and the politics and economics of global warming. Not without controversy surrounding the validity and accuracy of the film's message, undeniably one result of the film was a dramatic increase of interest and awareness of global warming. Gore's subsequent concert for change and the awarding of the Nobel Peace Prize has enhanced the visibility of the message. A second external factor is the ever-rising price at the gas pump. Hybrid cars are better for the environment, but given today's high gasoline prices, they are also better on the pocketbook. No doubt these work hand in hand.

- *Competitive factors:* In October 2005, Lee Scott, CEO of Wal-Mart, gave a speech titled "Twenty-First Century Leadership" in which he outlined the company's short- and long-term commitment to make zero waste, use 100 percent renewable energy, and sell sustainable products. Through several initiatives, Wal-Mart set in motion a trend that was quickly adopted by other retailers and is raising the bar for what it means to be green. In November 2007, Wal-Mart released its first Environmental Report outlining the behemoth retailer's progress toward its goals. The report was received with mixed feelings because some groups feel that no matter what Wal-Mart does to offset its negative impact, it can never do enough. What Wal-Mart did accomplish was to bring the issues of Greentailing to the masses, raising awareness among consumers, suppliers, and other corporations.

- *Internal factors:* Many companies embrace being green because it is the right thing to do. And they have done it well in advance of publicity and any obvious economic gain. This includes early pioneers like Gary Hirshberg at Stonyfield Farm and Ray Anderson, CEO of Interface, the large flooring supplier, who indicates he had an "ecological epiphany" after reading Paul Hawken's book *The Ecology of Commerce*, leading his company toward a more sustainable footprint.

- *Consumer:* Clearly the consumer has changed. From significant demographic factors to behavioral changes and shifting of priorities, consumers are willing to take new factors into consideration when they purchase items or determine which retailers they want to shop.

Whatever the ultimate contributors, Greentailing does appear to be here to stay.

GREENTAILERS ABROAD

Consumers are energetically seeking Greentailers to shop; employees want to work for Greentailers, and management has heightened green on its list of priorities. But where is this likely to lead? Since many British and other European companies are slightly ahead of U.S. companies in terms of Greentailing, we can use their experiences to help us look ahead to see the benefits, as well as the challenges.

Companies in the United Kingdom have made corporate social responsibility (CSR), a high priority. Marks & Spencer, the British retailer of clothing, food, and home products, has committed to CSR. The company's approach to CSR is based on its strong tradition and, according to the company's web site, integral in all that they do. The company's viewpoint is as follows: "Our founders believed that building good relationships with employees, suppliers, and wider society was the best guarantee of long-term success. This remains the backbone of our approach to CSR."

Marks & Spencer first published information on environmental issues in leaflets in 1990, which by 1997 grew into

20-page brochures. The company began publishing comprehensive reports on CSR in 2003 with its "Corporate Social Responsibility Review." Since that time, the company has issued CSR reports alongside its annual reports. Marks & Spencer continues to evolve as CSR issues do, and in January 2008, the company announced Plan A ("because there is no Plan B"), which is their five-year, 100-point eco-plan to be more sustainable and kinder to the environment. There are "Five Pillars" to the plan:

1. Become carbon neutral,
2. Send no waste to landfills,
3. Extend sustainable sourcing,
4. Help improve the lives of people in our supply chain, and
5. Help customers and employees live a healthier lifestyle.

Each pillar has its own set of goals, and Marks & Spencer lays out progress for each goal on its web site. Consumers can also use the site to read about how they can achieve similar goals in their own lives.

Like Marks & Spencer, Sainsbury's, a leading U.K. food retailer, credits its history and tradition for its commitment to corporate social responsibility. Their five guiding principles in this regard are:

1. The best for food and health,
2. Sourcing with integrity,

3. Respect for our environment,

4. Make a positive difference in our community, and

5. A great place to work.

Sainsbury's initiatives include its commitment to selling 100 percent fair trade bananas, improving the lives of farmers, and the company's "Bags for Life" program, which saves 50 million plastic bags from entering landfills annually.

Tesco, Britain's largest retailer, has long expressed clear core values of "no-one tries harder for customers" and "treat people how we like to be treated." Such values align well and characterize the company's approach to CSR. Tesco focuses on four key areas of CSR:

1. *Economy:* Using our strengths to deliver unbeatable value,

2. *Environment:* Working with our customers to help the environment,

3. *Society:* Playing our part in local communities, and

4. *Charities and fund-raising:* Supporting good causes.

Tesco is developing a system of carbon labeling that measures each of the company's over 70,000 products' carbon footprints (a measure of contribution to global warming), a very complicated task that only a company the size of Tesco could accomplish. In April 2008, Tesco began testing the carbon labels on twenty store items from potato chips to lightbulbs, however no timetable to expand the program has been set. While the latest updates suggest that the system was, at a minimum, ambitious, Tesco is at least making some headway on what is a very multifaceted and often misunderstood issue.

WHAT ARE THE KEY ELEMENTS OF GREENTAILING?

While there a number of ways to be green, we believe there are four key elements of a successful Greentailer:

1. Think green,
2. Act green,
3. Sell green, and
4. Convey green.

Think Green

A word used a lot in company mission statements and CSR reports is *sustainability*. What sustainability means to consumers is difficult to define and Greentailers often create their own definition of how it pertains to their business.

> Sustainability is a system utilizing renewable resources that meets the requirements of the present without compromising the requirements of future generations or disrupting present or future environmental balance.

That is a mouthful; however, sustainability is how a lot of Greentailers sum up their environmental and social green efforts.

Green as a Mission and Core Value

Whole Foods Market's vision is of a sustainable future, which is incorporated in its company mission statement:

Our children and grandchildren will be living in a world that values human creativity, diversity, and individual choice. Businesses will harness human and material resources without devaluing the integrity of the individual or the planet's ecosystems. Companies, governments, and institutions will be held accountable for their actions.[4]

Whole Foods Market is generally considered the paragon of all things green. Yet, it is easy to take issue with many of their actions. While promoting local sourcing in a major way, they still rely heavily on imported goods to fill their mix. Their stores are greener nowadays but there is plenty of flash and glitter. They are hardly earthy outposts. That said, we suspect most customers want them that way. Practically speaking, most customers want to have their cake (with imported Belgian chocolate in beautiful well-lit cases) and eat it, too. While Whole Foods may indeed lead the charge, they will also be a target for the fervent environmentalists who see plenty of room for improvement.

Green Advocates or Officers

Most all of the successful Greentailers have a point person for green, with varying responsibilities, but nonetheless a person or team responsible for overseeing green activities. In a July 3, 2007, *New York Times* article, "Companies Giving Green an Office," Claudia Deutsch writes,

The corporate roster of "chiefs" used to be pretty short: chief executive, chief financial officer and, maybe, chief operating officer. Then came the chief marketing and technology officers. Now, the so-called C-Level Suite is swelling again—this time, with chief sustainability officers.[5]

Interestingly, these so-called environmentalist chiefs come from all different backgrounds and as a result are influencing all parts of the business. Maybe one day students will major in corporate sustainability.

Act Green

A tangible way to convey greenness is through the infrastructure in which you operate. Several retailers have taken to building and/or retrofitting stores to optimize energy efficiency and through in-store marketing point out these efficiencies. The establishment of the U.S. Green Building Council's Leadership in Energy and Environmental Design (LEED) rating system in 1998 has led to tangible and measurable standards for design, construction, and operation of green buildings. LEED Certification is tailored for specific projects and can be achieved through standards with varying degrees of strictness, from Certified to Silver, Gold, and Platinum. Unfortunately, there are very few certified LEED projects to date in retail. But that doesn't mean that considerable efforts aren't being taken. Many retailers are using eco-prototype stores as a testing ground for high energy-efficient lighting, rainwater recycling, recycled content building materials, and high-efficiency HVAC systems. Companies including Target, Best Buy, Office Depot, and many more are opening LEED certified stores. Every week we learn of another LEED retail project. The LEED Green Building Rating System was created to encourage and accelerate global adoption of sustainable green building and development practices. (see Table 3.2).

While LEED certification is a rather extreme step that is just now being embraced, several environmentally friendly building practices are making their way into the mainstream, particularly in energy usage levels. Changing to energy-efficient lighting, energy-efficient fixtures, and the use of more sustainable building materials is becoming commonplace. Again, this is another example where retailers can do good and save money in the long term. There has been relatively fast adoption of green practices that also happen to save money.

Another area of acting green is in transportation. A number of companies have begun the process of shifting their vehicle fleet to more natural burning fuels and utilizing recycled vegetable oils. At the Mall of America, internal maintenance trucks smell distinctly of french fries because they have utilized recycled product. Safeway is converting

Table 3.2 Retailers Who Have Achieved LEED Certification

Retailer or Retail Development	Location	Date Certified	Certification Level
Recreational Equipment, Inc. (REI)	Portland, OR	09/30/2004	Gold
Happy Feet Plus, Inc.	Clearwater, FL	10/15/2004	Gold
Giant Eagle Market #229	Brunswick, OH	12/06/2004	Certified
Winnipeg Mountain Equipment Co-Op	Winnipeg, MB	12/20/2004	Gold
Chicago Merchandise Mart—Neocon	Chicago, IL	06/08/2005	Gold
Shaw's Superstore	Worcester, MA	09/01/2005	Certified
Whole Foods Market	Sarasota, FL	09/09/2005	Silver
Lowe's of S.W. Austin	Austin, TX	03/06/2006	Gold
La Regional Showroom	Santa Monica, CA	03/15/2006	Gold
The Home Depot (North Hill)	Calgary, AB	03/27/2006	Certified
Abercorn Common	Savannah, GA	04/19/2006	Silver
Wainwright Bank	Brookline, MA	08/10/2006	Silver
The Water Street Market	Corvallis, OR	08/10/2006	Certified
Recreational Equipment, Inc. (REI)	Pittsburgh, PA	08/10/2006	Silver
Target (Mckinley Park)	Chicago, IL	08/25/2006	Certified
Abercorn Common-Shops 600	Savannah, GA	02/01/2007	Silver
Giant Eagle Market #40	Pittsburgh, PA	03/22/2007	Silver
Helios House	Los Angeles, CA	04/02/2007	Certified
Natural Body—Ryan Park	Ashburn, VA	04/22/2007	Silver

(*Continued*)

Table 3.2   *(Continued)*

Retailer or Retail Development	Location	Date Certified	Certification Level
Wainwright Bank Newton Centre	Newton, MA	05/23/2007	Gold
PCC—Redmond	Redmond, WA	07/16/2007	Gold
Knoll Philadelphia	Atlanta, GA	08/07/2007	Silver
Nau	Boulder, CO	10/01/2007	Gold
Target (Peterson Avenue)	Chicago, IL	10/17/2007	Certified
Milliken Carpet Showroom	Chicago, IL	10/31/2007	Gold
Meijer Store #233	Allen Park, MI	11/19/2007	Silver
The Home Depot (South Loop)	Chicago, IL	12/20/2007	Certified

Source: U.S. Green Building Council, www.usgbc.org (retrieved January 22, 2008).

its fleet, reducing fuel costs by as much as 20 percent. Again, achieving green isn't simple, and trading one resource (gas) for another (corn) leads to further arguments on what's best.

Greening the Supply Chain: Supplier Relationships and Practices

A Greentailer's relationship with its supplier is a dynamic one. For many years, suppliers have had one goal (if not an enormously difficult one)—make it better and make it cheaper. Now, the advent of Greentailing suggests a new dynamic: Suppliers beware—the movement toward green will inevitably have significant repercussions and potentially greater costs. If retailers change their standards—for products, shipping, packaging, quality assurance, and so on, suppliers will inevitably feel the pain.

A dynamic example of sweeping change in the supply chain concerns the adoption of "ultra packaging" in the laundry detergent category. Beginning with Unilever's All Mighty and Wal-Mart, ultra sizes were introduced into the United States marketplace. Subsequently, Wal-Mart announced that the company will phase out all other forms of detergent, creating a groundswell of innovation that should reduce packaging cost and waste across the entire category. Ultra packaging has been a great environmental achievement, spurred on by a powerful retailer that forced huge changes across the supply chain.

But, manufacturers with established facilities can't turn on a dime. The costs involved in developing more sustainable approaches will be considerable, despite the good intentions.

Green can quickly become red, with all of the negative repercussions. As one red example, the 2007 Sears Wish Book catalog was printed on paper from a supplier that sourced from environmentally sensitive areas in Canada. Nonprofit groups staged demonstrations in 70 North American cities against the company citing that the four million catalogs killed 162,000 trees from an endangered caribou habitat in Ontario's boreal forest.

Packaging

Greentailers recognize the importance of reducing unnecessary packaging. One example of this trend is the increase in the use of reusable bags as replacements for plastic shopping bags. San Francisco was the first city to ban plastic grocery bags at large supermarkets and pharmacies. Regulators in other cities are considering similar bans.

Herein lies a perfect example of contradiction and poor Greentailing when retailers are most vulnerable. A green message doesn't ring clear if you throw all the organic lettuce, fair trade coffee, and made-from-recycled-material kitchen gloves into a plastic bag. That is, unless you offer recycling services for that bag or an option to purchase a reusable bag as alternatives to throwing them away. Another example is sending out expensive catalogs and/or marketing material—direct marketers understand that more catalogs in more customers' hands leads to greater sales. But, it also leads to far greater waste. The actions and messages of green need to be consistently integrated and still enable retailers to meet their business goals.

Greentailing and Reduce, Reuse, Recycle

Obviously, retailers and consumers can do a more effective job of creating less waste and better utilizing existing materials. Publix Super Markets, simple act of offering a place to recycle plastic bags was one of the more frequently cited green practices in our research. Responsible recycling programs are green friendly and can be a significant money saver, too.

Mall of America is a fantastic example of utilizing recycling to do what's right and save significant money as well. The largest mall in the United States is a mini-city unto itself and a model of efficiency and cost savings. Mall of America management chose to recycle from the beginning and reuse and recycle just about everything imaginable. Their tenants get into the act as well—being responsible recyclers keeps their common area maintenance (CAM) charges down. The mall sponsored an electronics recycling program that had to close prematurely due to overwhelming consumer demand (and overwhelming amounts of electronics to recycle).

There is a depressing downside to Mall of America's enviable greenness. The one area where they don't recycle is the consumer-facing portions of their business. Every effort to get the customers to do some simple sorting of waste has met with failure. Perhaps the consumer is not ready to act as green as they say. Or, perhaps, as our next chapter examines, the average consumer talks a better green game than they play.

Sell Green

Just as determining what makes a retailer green is difficult, so is creating an understanding of what constitutes a green product. In fact, any criteria used to create green seem subject to their own debate. Every word is loaded and there is no shortage of controversy. Whether retailers or suppliers are well-intended or whether products are rushed out into the market for the sake of positive environmental relations (ER), it is a slippery slope to navigate. The loser in all of this is the consumer who wants simply answers and retailers who may shoot themselves in the foot through unintentional greenwashing.

We have found that products may be considered green in many ways, but here are some words to look for:

- *Organic:* The only defined and regulated green product
- *Natural:* Presumably comprising organic and/or nontoxic ingredients
- *Local:* Or locally sourced
- *Sustainable:* A loaded word, to be sure. And one that is hotly contested among hardcore environmentalists
- *Ethically sourced:* Back to the source and often linked to fair trade
- *Environmentally friendly:* Made with minimal or recycled packaging and does not damage the environment
- *Minimal waste:* Reusable
- *Carbon offset:* The product's negative impact has been offset with credits
- *Nontoxic materials:* Natural and Earth friendly

There are some definitions and regulations around these terms but most remain loosely defined at best. Environmentalists tend to be like economists, finding at least three sides to every issue (and term). Organic food, as an example, is now certified by the U.S. government, but terms like *natural* are not and are loosely thrown around by marketers. And, is it more important to be organic than it is to be local? While organically produced goods are theoretically better, they still may be transported great distances and still consume resources. Sustainable is often a matter of great debate, particularly as it relates to a product being environmentally friendly or creating less waste. Ethical sourcing, we believe, will grow tremendously in future importance because it relates to a myriad of societal factors, from living wages, humane working conditions, and fair trade.

Confused? So are we, even as we learn and study more. Imagine how consumers feel as they try to navigate their way through this maze. While organic food products are certified, organic apparel or beauty products are not (yet). You might see a shirt labeled organic that was made with organic cotton. But what about the dyes, or stitching, or labeling? There are looser regulations regarding these areas. And that same organic shirt may have been made in less-than-socially-friendly working conditions. Tracing the origins of an eco-friendly product can lead to a complicated labyrinth.

Our role is not to be environmentalists. Intent is important. Consumers will see through blatantly false claims and a retailer and supplier can end up getting burned for a green product that isn't truly green.

Organic

The evolution of organic is important because it may illustrate how concrete product definitions come to be. Organic products have grown significantly over the past decade or so and have served as an introduction to Greentailing for a number of retailers. The Organic Trade Association estimates that organic food sales comprised over $16 billion in

Table 3.3   Total Foods and Organic Foods Consumer Sales and Penetration, 1997–2006

Year	Organic Food Sales ($ million)	Organic Food Sales Growth (%)	Total Food Sales ($ million)	Organic Penetration (%)
1997	3,594	N/A	443,790	0.8
1998	4,286	19.2	454,140	0.9
1999	5,039	17.6	474,790	1.1
2000	6,100	21.0	498,380	1.2
2001	7,360	20.7	521,830	1.4
2002	8,625	17.3	530,612	1.6
2003	10,381	20.2	535,406	1.9
2004	11,902	14.6	544,141	2.2
2005	13,831	16.2	556,791	2.5
2006	16,718	20.9	598,136	2.8

Source: Organic Trade Association's manufacturer survey, 2006 and 2007.

2006 or approximately 3 percent of the overall food market. These numbers represent growth rates of approximately 15 percent to 20 percent a year (see Table 3.3).

Safeway has had tremendous success with its O organics private label program that comprised over $170 million in sales in 2006. In fact, O has been so successful for Safeway that the company is selling the products in foreign countries and extending the brand into foodservice. Mainstream brands from Campbells to Kelloggs to Kraft have introduced organic variations of their traditional products. Wal-Mart made a very visible public push for carrying more organics, though they seem to have pulled back from the effort recently. Organics, a tangible product manifestation of green, has grown for many reasons. A more discerning and concerned consumer is more conscious of what they are putting in their (and their children's) bodies. Not to be overlooked, however, is the fact that the price gap between conventionally grown and organic products is narrowing. Again, the paradox of green comes into play. As organic suppliers gear up to serve larger demand, many feel that the principles of organics become compromised.

From produce to cleaning supplies, consumers have the option of consciously paying more for a product that is good for you, of higher quality, and presumably good for the environment. Several brands have quickly emerged as trusted sources of organic products, like Method. Whole Foods Markets are a source for organic goods and exemplify consumer willingness to pay more for organic and high quality.

Local

More and more products are being marketed as local these days. Local green is environmentally friendly for three key reasons: 1.) Local implies small, and that implies natural production processes, which means pesticide-free, organic, and natural. 2.) Local means shorter and less costly transport, and less carbon emissions from sourcing from a more distant location. 3.) Local means supporting fellow neighbors and the local economy. There is a significant trust factor that comes into play when a product is locally grown or made. It seems to be associated with a local standard and associated with the idea that a local source adheres to the same quality standard a consumer is familiar with and surrounded by.

A recent example that justifies the local focus was the massive safety recalls of Chinese manufactured toys with excessive lead levels. Companies like Mattel recalled close to 10 million toys and alerted Americans to the threat of Chinese manufactured toys or parts, which account for between 70 percent and 80 percent of all toys on U.S. shelves. Worried parents, searching for a solution, redirected their dollars toward hard-to-find U.S. made toys, and often locally made, old-fashioned toys. Companies like Whittle Shortline Railroad toy company of Louisiana, Missouri; Holgate Toys of Bradford, Pennsylvania; and Hatfield, Pennsylvania-based K'Nex Toys saw a surge of sales and staffed accordingly to meet the demand. Will consumers pay more for local, reversing the long-running trend toward global sourcing?

Convey Green

Like the awakening of individual consciousness toward the environment, corporations are also receiving wake-up calls or are proactively attempting to change their paths. Obviously, CSR extends well beyond the environment. A utopian, if unachievable definition of CSR would mean assuring that the end consumer can have confidence that no person and no place are negatively impacted by the products and services for sale. For a Greentailer, CSR is communicated through its stores, its products, and its people.

Obviously, running a for-profit corporation requires a retailer to balance the need to make a profit and remain competitive in the marketplace, while trying to adhere to socially responsible practices. This is the essence of business and the essence of social responsibility. A good corporate citizen must provide adequate returns to the stakeholders of the company, be a good neighbor to its community, a good employer to its associate and offer great products to the consumer. There will never be a firm right answer on providing that balance.

Why the sudden attention to CSR? Most corporations have traditionally relied on government to set policy and then (grudgingly, at times) follow it. The government sets minimum wages for employees yet these wages are embarrassingly low and don't adequately provide for families. Many companies pay more due to competitive conditions or the understanding that a more satisfied workforce is a better one. Offering health-care benefits to workers also falls under the same area—it is a significant social issue and a battleground for companies as they fight rising costs. When it comes to areas surrounding green, progressive companies will get ahead of the curve, enacting their own changes ahead of mandates. Or, more importantly, become active voices in the debate.

Charity

Charity, as a way to convey greenness, usually means a percentage of sales go toward a cause, which can be anything that is socially responsible. More broadly, charity can also be used as a way to offset or draw attention away from less green practices. The Barneys' 2007 Holiday Catalog "Have a Green Holiday" exemplified this. Interspersed throughout the catalog were green products with "philanthropic gestures." The actual catalog, printed on glossy, heavy stock paper—although it didn't appear so—was printed on paper that was certified by the Forest Stewardship Council, using soybean-based inks and paper containing 30 percent postconsumer waste material. The high-end assortment of clothing and accessories helped Barneys' customers feel good about purchasing from the catalog since a portion of the proceeds went to a good cause. Not everything in the catalog was green though, and this puts into question how devoted Barneys is to Greentailing or if they were capitalizing on the green trend. If the message isn't integrated and consistent, it is in question.

Charity has broader implications tied to assuaging the consumer's guilt over consumption and providing subtle or not-so-subtle links to corporations and charity. There are multiple forms of charitable contributions in place today. They raise the question of just how active retailers should be. Activity ranges from the passive but strongly philanthropic approach of Target (5 percent of pretax profits) to the questionable practice of asking the customer for a donation at the register. While charitable approaches have become well established, the more they tie into a retailer's core mission, the better. A strong example is Petco asking consumers to "round up" their bill with proceeds going to the Humane Society (a pretty tight match-up between customer and charity) to the disparate (Safeway donating to prostate or breast cancer causes). While noble, the direct tie to a particular cause is lacking. Better yet, the actions of Buffalo Exchange (save a bag, save some money) establish a more direct, cause-and-effect approach. The principles of T.A.S.C. (Think, Act, Sell, and Convey Green) establish the foundation of an effective Greentailing plan.

CHAPTER FOUR

THE CONSUMER'S VIEW ON GREEN

I n retailing, there is really only one reliable form of consumer opinion—where and how they spend their money. We mention this because consumers will often say one thing to a researcher and then spend their money in a very different way. We've heard countless consumers pine about the lost tradition of in-town stores and personalized service, then turn around and spend their money at Wal-Mart or Home Depot. Of course, that doesn't stop companies from spending millions and millions of dollars on consumer research to ask customers what they might do in the future. And we do exactly the same thing on behalf of our clients on a fairly regular basis. But it has taught us to look at research results with a grain of salt when it comes to predicting the future. It's not that consumers aren't telling a version of what they believe, but purchase intent and actual purchasing are two very different things.

That preamble leads us to this chapter of the consumer's view on green. We have looked at dozens of studies over the past several months that track what consumers are saying about green. If you took any of these studies at face value, retailers should be rushing to "green" their operations immediately. Apparently, there are vast numbers of consumers who are willing to do anything to be green. Yet, the empirical data on the sales of green goods (recycled product paper goods, hybrid cars, organic cotton shirts, etc.) suggest that the market is considerably smaller than you might think. Who sells more paper towels, Bounty or Seventh Generation?

We conducted our own research study at the beginning of 2008 to create our own set of data concerning consumers and their attitudes toward green. We polled over 1,000 consumers across geography, age, and income to understand their perceptions. While not shocking in what they said, we believe there are a number of clues that a savvy retailer or supplier can pick up on to help manage their green efforts in the future.

GREEN PRACTICES

When asked to talk to their actual green behavior, just 12 percent of the population actively consider or purchase green merchandise (Table 4.1). An additional 47 percent say they will occasionally consider or purchase green-oriented merchandise. Effectively 60 percent of the population has green in their overall consideration set while 40 percent do not. This is a fairly substantial piece of the consumer audience.

Table 4.1   Impact of Environmental or Green Concerns on Shopping/ Purchasing Behavior

Consider or Purchase/ Shop Green . . .	*Percent*
Actively	12
Occasionally	47
Rarely	26
Never	14

How the 12 percent who say they are "active" green purchasers correlate with any actual buying behavior.

When asked how retailers are doing in their efforts to be environmentally friendly, 54 percent said not enough and 38 percent said about the right amount (Table 4.2). Retailers are clearly getting credit for making an effort. And to those 8 percent who said "too much," we'll see you at Dick Cheney's family reunion.

Interestingly, while many retailers are considered to be making a decent effort at being green, they are not doing a particularly good job of educating the consumer on what they are doing. Just 6 percent of consumers rated retailers as excellent or very good at educating consumer on green, while over half believed they are below satisfactory or poor (Table 4.3). It is critical to think of the barrage of

Table 4.2   Are Retailers Doing Enough to Be Environmentally Friendly or Green?

Retailers Are Doing . . .	*Percent*
Not enough	54
About the right amount	38
Too much	8

Table 4.3   Educating Consumers about Environmentally Friendly or Green Activities

Retailer Rating	Percent
5—Excellent	2
4—Very good	4
3—Satisfactory	43
2—Below satisfactory	42
1—Poor	10
Average rating	2.5

communications that face consumers every day and realize that green is not breaking out from the crowd. It also should be noted that efforts at consumer education will need to go on for some time before the messages begin to stick.

What retailers exemplify greenness? Only 24 percent of the population could mention a particular green retailer on an unaided basis (Table 4.4). This is another good indicator that there is a lot of hype but little substance to date, at

Table 4.4   Retailers Who Exemplify Green Practices

Retailers	Percent
Whole Foods	21
Wal-Mart	20
Trader Joe's	11
Target	9
Publix	4
Home Depot	2
Costco	2
Body Shop	2
Staples	2
BP	2

Respondents provided retailer names without aid or prompting.

251 respondents (24% of sample) named a retailer.

least as far as the mainstream consumer is concerned. Not surprisingly, on some reflection, two seemingly disparate retailers, Whole Foods and Wal-Mart, jump to the front of the Greentailer pack. We suspect Whole Foods made it due to their company-wide stance on Greentailing and Wal-Mart for their efforts and visibility on all things retail. Both are profiled later in this book.

About a third of the population (36 percent) report that they are changing their purchasing behavior to shop retailers who are implementing greener practices. While the list of admired retailers is short, a green reputation could be very good business for manufacturers and suppliers.

Although nearly 60 percent of the population said they actively or occasionally consider green in their purchasing habits, just 49 percent report making a purchase. Other studies we have looked at suggest that compact flourescent light (CFL) bulbs and energy efficient appliances ENERGY STAR® are early green front-runners.

A major concern from our research is the perceived performance of green products. Our survey suggests that consumer satisfaction with green purchases has not been very high. Only 13 percent rated the performance of green products excellent and nearly half said satisfactory. As marketers know, satisfactory doesn't breed loyalty.

Green, in fact, may have a negative halo when it concerns product quality. Consumers seem to feel good about being green, but suspect that they must sacrifice something in quality, styling, or performance. Only 49 percent of the consumers surveyed purchased a product in the past year that was specifically green. Brands that want to be green must walk a very fine line on the environmentally friendly positioning versus perceived diminution of quality (Table 4.5). As going green becomes more mainstream, this effect will hopefully become minimized.

One of our real curiosities is trying to understand what's behind Greentailing 2.0. As we suspected, green is being driven by a variety of factors. But, clearly, the threat of global warming and the very real cost of fuel and oil emerge as the two big drivers (Table 4.6).

When we then asked consumers what they were personally doing to respond to the green movement, a fairly standard list developed. More environmentally friendly products, reduction in energy usage, and reduced used of packaging made the list. Consuming less—that paradox of Greentailing—has yet to emerge (Table 4.7).

Perhaps the most critical finding in our entire study is contained in consumer answers to the question of how much more they are willing to pay to be green. The answer—not much! A full 40 percent say they are willing to pay nothing at all, which corresponds nicely to the percentage of population

Table 4.5   Performance of Environmentally Friendly or Green Product

Product Performance Rating	Percent
5—Excellent	13
4—Very good	32
3—Satisfactory	52
2—Below satisfactory	4
1—Poor	0
Average rating	3.5

Table 4.6   Why You Purchase or Shop More Environmentally Friendly or Green Products/Retailers

Influencing Factors	Influenced Decision (%)	Main Reason for Decision (%)
News/information on global warming	65	30
Increase in price of fuel/oil	66	17
News/information on pollution	57	13
Educational efforts by organizations promoting greener lifestyles	36	12
Educational efforts by product manufacturers	32	6
Notoriety and popularity of the Al Gore movie *The Inconvenient Truth*	26	6
Educational efforts by retailers	23	3
Educational efforts by universities	22	3
Hurricane Katrina	21	3
Educational efforts by government entities	18	1

Respondents whose purchasing practices have been influenced.

Table 4.7   Types of Environmental or Green Practices Adopted

Environmental or Green Practices	Percent
Purchase more environmentally friendly or green products for personal use	77
Purchase products that reduce energy usage	77
Reducing usage of bags and packaging materials	64
Purchasing at stores that have adapted environmentally friendly practices	38
Purchase more environmentally friendly or green products for gifts	32
Purchasing at stores that donate a percentage of their sales to environmental causes	19

Table 4.8   How Much More Are You Willing to Pay for Environmentally Friendly or Green Products?

I will pay ...	Percent
Nothing	40
5 percent more	27
10 percent more	18
15 percent more	7
20 percent more	5
25 percent more	1
30 percent more	1
Median additional (among those willing to pay more)	5.8

that said they really don't care (Table 4.8). But 45 percent of consumers were only willing to pay between 5 percent to 10 percent more to be greener. Clearly percentages mean different things for different product categories. 10 percent more on a can of peas (okay, organic peas) is a whole lot less in absolute terms than 10 percent more for a hybrid car. Regardless, the number is quite small (and not near enough to bank on society becoming significantly green). And it is even smaller still when you think about the real-world consequences. If consumers, in their idealized survey selves—are only saying they are willing to spend 5 percent to 10 percent more, the reality is that the real number is probably even lower. Organic food sales didn't really take off until price gaps between conventional and organic products narrowed substantially.

When consumers were asked what green practices were most important, recycling and operating in an energy efficient manner were the top two responses. Interestingly, many retailers are beginning to adopt simple programs for

Table 4.9   **Environmental or Green Practices Expected to
Grow in Importance to You**

Environmental or Green Practices	*Percent*
Recycling services	66
Operate in a manner to save energy	65
Use sustainable materials and packing	64
Inform customers about how to be more environmentally friendly	38
Use fair trade purchasing practices	34
Support local environmental or green causes	33
Offer organic ingredients or materials	31
Do not expect any practices to grow in importance	11

the recycling of bags, and it won't be long before bag usage itself comes under attack (consuming less works better every time) as it has in most other parts of the world. Sustainable packaging was next in importance, followed by education and information. How green affects the actual buying and constitution of products was considered less important—the use of organic materials and fair trade practices finished lower. Again, in areas where paying more for green would directly impact consumers, their enthusiasm was considerably lower. This is supported as well in Table 4.9 that details what practices consumers expect to grow in importance in the coming years.

WHERE THE RUBBER HITS THE ROAD—WHAT MATTERS MOST

We are starting to see new stores pop up that are expressly green-oriented. And, we are certainly seeing an influx of green-oriented marketing materials. This is all consistent with a growing trend and consistent with what is obviously becoming a significant sociological and cultural issue. We are clearly going to become greener, for a variety of both practical and ethical reasons. Yet, when you review the research, a few facts jump out:

- Although a high percentage of customers say they consider buying green, relatively few do so today both in practice and in our research.
- Green products have a stigma of lower quality associated with them.
- Consumers are only willing to pay a slight premium to be green (and probably not enough to justify the added costs).
- Consumers want their stores and manufacturers to be greener in practices, but they are not necessarily willing to pay for it as it works down into the supply chain.
- The tried-and-true reasons for selecting a store still dominate the consumer's decision-making process. When consumers were asked to judge how they choose a store, a relatively predictable list of attributes emerges: prices, merchandise quality, selection, customer service, and ease of shopping all are more important than a retailer being environmentally friendly.

In Table 4.10, we look at those attributes across a variety of store types—department stores, discount stores, apparel specialty stores, supermarkets, consumer electronics, office

Table 4.10 Attribute Importance in Selecting Favorite Store by Store Type

Type of Store	Prices Charged	Merchandise Quality	Selection	Customer Service	Ease of Shopping	Store Is Environmentally Friendly
Department	4.3	4.3	4.1	4.0	3.9	2.9
Discount	4.5	4.2	4.1	4.0	3.8	3.0
Apparel specialty	4.3	4.2	4.2	4.0	4.0	3.0
Supermarket/grocery	4.5	4.4	4.3	4.2	4.0	3.1
Consumer electronics	4.5	4.4	4.3	4.1	4.0	2.9
Home improvement	4.5	4.4	4.3	4.1	4.1	3.0
Office supply	4.4	4.3	4.2	4.0	4.0	3.0
Pet supply	4.4	4.3	4.2	4.0	3.9	3.0

5 = Very important; 1 = Not at all important.

supplies, and pet food. In all areas, environmentally friendly received only average ratings for importance.

Greentailing may be the wave of the future, but customers are slow to change long-ingrained habits. Retailers should be greener, but they can't forget low prices, high-quality, extensive selections, ease of shopping, and great customer service.

CHAPTER FIVE

GREENTAILING IN ACTION— CASE STUDIES

How is Greentailing manifesting itself in the real world of retail? Can a compelling case be made that green not only produces goodwill but results in higher long-term profitability? From single store operators to the world's largest retailer, everyone is dealing with green in their own unique ways. We examined retailers and suppliers to detail what they are doing and see if we couldn't develop some universal truths around their activities. We looked at a very small, start-up retailer in Chicago and the world's largest retail company, Wal-Mart.

What we found emphasizes the groundswell of activity that surrounds green, as well as a significant diversity in direction as to the right approach. It's clear that we are at Greentailing's nascent development—both the number and types of green activities will undoubtedly multiply many times over in the next decade. We also found that there is literally no end in sight to the richness available in potential material. On a daily basis, new Greentailing practices from supermarkets, discounters, home stores, office supply stores, and a variety of suppliers across all industries surfaced, and a growing stream of green entrepreneurs are appearing.

Here, then, is a sampling of current Greentailing practices in action. As with any area that is in its nascent development, the consumer is going to be forced to navigate a maze of approaches, and marketing claims. It will be difficult for consumers to distinguish perception from reality and will take genuine and integrated efforts from suppliers and retailers to bring clarity.

APPAREL, HOME, AND SPECIALTY RETAIL

Buffalo Exchange—Renewable Green

The easiest way to be green is to simply consume less. Or consumers could reuse products that have already been created and already exist in the marketplace. At first glance, Buffalo Exchange might simply be viewed as a thrift shop— nothing too green about that on the surface. But with deeper analysis, it is an excellent place to start the discussion on green in retailing.

Buffalo Exchange works to protect the environment by reusing and recycling clothing. According to the U.S. Environmental Protection Agency, postconsumer textile products represent 5 percent or 11.8 million tons of total municipal solid waste (MSW). The average U.S. consumer throws away 68 pounds of clothing and textiles per year. And according to the Council for Textile Recycling, textile recycling prevents 2.5 billion pounds of postconsumer textile product waste from entering the solid waste stream annually, which translates into 10 pounds of clothing and textiles for every person in the United States. Fact number one—we have created a disposable society, from the food we consume to the clothes we wear. Obviously, consuming less, reusing or recycling in a more conscientious manner would go a long way to greening America.

Buffalo Exchange first opened its doors in 1974 in Tucson, Arizona, with a 450-square-foot store devoted to recycling through buying, selling, and trading clothing items and accessories. Located near the University of Arizona campus, Buffalo Exchange led the resale fashion industry as the first store of its kind. It differentiated itself by selecting only quality, fashionable items and offering used clothes at low prices in a clean store with a boutique atmosphere.

Since its inception, the store has grown to 33 company-owned stores and 3 franchises with over $48 million a year in sales. It has presence in 13 states offering a product mix of new and used clothing and accessories that can be purchased outright or through trade. The original founders, Kerstin and Spencer Block still own and operate the company-owned stores along with daughter Rebecca.

With the advent of fast-fashion retailers, wardrobes are increasingly more disposable. Buffalo Exchange is high on the Greentailing scale in that it has low carbon dioxide emissions because it does not manufacture apparel goods. As a secondary market, the stores capitalize on the idiom, "One man's trash is another man's treasure" offering a solution to the growing problem of postconsumer textile product contributing to landfill waste.

In addition to providing a venue to recycle clothing and apparel, Buffalo Exchange helps the environment through several programs including the Tokens for Bags program. The Tokens for Bags program encourages shoppers to accept a token instead of a bag for purchases, with each token representing a 5 cent donation to a charity of the customer's choice.

In conjunction with Earth Day, all Buffalo Exchange stores have a sale with all items selling for one dollar and the proceeds are used to benefit an environmental cause. Since 1997, Buffalo Exchange has raised over $211,000 for environmental causes through its Dollar Sale program. Through a partnership with the Humane Society of the United States Coats for Cubs program, Buffalo Exchange accepts donations of real fur apparel, including trims, accessories, and shearling that are then utilized to provide bedding and comfort to orphaned and injured wildlife. As a result, less fur apparel enters the municipal solid waste stream and is instead reused for animals in need.

Through its recycling of clothing and accessories and partnerships with environmental cause-oriented organizations, Buffalo Exchange gains the trust of its customers as a Greentailer who practices what it preaches.

Pivot Boutique—A Green Entrepreneur

A pivot is a point around which something turns, and owner Jessa Brinkmeyer hopes that shoppers will be turned on by the idea of dressing green. Pivot Boutique, Chicago's first destination eco-boutique, opened in September 2007 and gained attention from the start, but not as many shoppers as hoped. Located in the predominantly industrial Fulton Market District, the space is filled with recycled furniture, fluorescent bulbs, and toxin-free paint. The interior was designed by a local artist who used recycled materials to create unique custom furniture and fixtures. Brinkmeyer has collections from over 25 eco-friendly designers of women's apparel and accessories, which adds to the draw for customer's seeking fashionable green goods.

Pivot is admirable in its consistency. All of the store's merchandise qualifies as eco-friendly, carefully edited and approved by the hands-on owner. When you step into the store, the recycled and artistically crafted fixtures pop against the white walls in the loft-like space. A note on the counter reads something like, "To control waste, shopping bags are available by request. Please consider the environment when making your decision." Also, a percentage of sales go to Growing Home, a nonprofit organization that provides organic farming jobs to the underserved.

Pivot must deal with the myriad of challenges facing any start up or entrepreneurial business. Is the location, on the edge of more mainstream shopping, right? Is the "boutique pricing" a potential obstacle for their customers, whose pocketbooks may not be as "green" as their intentions? Does a stigma still remain reconciling the notion of fashion and quality with green?

There will be plenty of Pivots out there breaking ground in creating a fully integrated effort between product, policy, and the in-store environment. It is exciting, if not also more than a bit scary, to be on the leading edge. The snowball effect of consumer acceptance will also no doubt lead to more suppliers, lower prices, and a larger business that is "sustainable" on all levels.

Nau—And the Dangers of Getting Ahead of the Curve

As of May 2, 2008, Nau announced that they were shuttering their operations, a victim of a confluence of factors including poor timing to start up a business. Left unsaid in their press release was that the concept was struggling to find customers as they balanced green and fashion. As disappointed as we were to see Nau close, it provides an unfortunate lesson in understanding profitable green—namely, you can't lose sight of the basics of how customers shop a category.

Nau, headquartered in Portland, Oregon, was a technical and lifestyle outdoor apparel retailer and may have represented the tipping point in green retailing. Nau was on the edge of Greentailing, and their reach promised to challenge the boundaries of how far green can go while still pursuing a profitable business model. While we love the concepts that Nau embraced, it certainly brings into question just how far a consumer will go to support a sustainable business.

Nau, which means "welcome" in Maori, had a unique business model built around sustainable business practices through integration of environmental, social, and economic factors and was "welcoming" a whole new way of designing, manufacturing, and selling products. Nau was founded in 2005 by an experienced team from the outdoor, fitness, and fashion retail industries including Patagonia, Nike, Adidas, and Cole Haan brands. The company marketed and sold its merchandise through five "webfront" stores in Oregon, Washington State, Colorado, Illinois, and California and its web site.

Nau believed the new measure for retail success was blending profitability with philanthropy. Their goal was "To demonstrate the highest levels of citizenship in everything we do: product creation, production, labor practices, the way we treat each other, environmental practices, and philanthropy."

They differed from traditional outdoor apparel retailers in three major ways. First, all products are made from recycled polyester, certified organic fabrics, and biodegradable corn fiber. The product designs feature subdued colors with a classic style that was meant to endure fashion trends and thus make for a sustainable wardrobe. They identified their three customer types as athletes, artists, and activists. The clothes served people who like to engage in outdoor activities, appreciate fine design, and who live responsible lives.

Second, Nau's product delivery mechanism of "webfronts" integrated e-commerce with traditional brick-and-mortar shopping with a digital approach to storytelling and brand building. Instead of encouraging in-store shopping, Nau offered free ground shipping and a 10 percent discount incentive to customers who ordered clothes online from in-store kiosks. The business standpoint of this was that they could showcase as many styles in a 2,000-square-foot store as would traditionally require 4,000 square feet of retail space. The company explained this approach saved on capital cost, overhead, lease costs, labor, and materials. They hoped the smaller webfront format would help them hit 72 percent gross margins, compared to the 45 percent to 60 percent gross margins of traditional retailers.

Third, Nau's Partners for Change program represented a new and unique for-profit, not for-profit partnership with 5 percent of every sale going to one of the environmental, social, or humanitarian partners of the customers choosing. Nau promoted all causes that each Partner for Change partic-ipant represented and integrated their causes into the stores. The in-store Product Information Tree allowed customers to learn about not only the products but also the Partners for Change participants and controlled the level of information they received.

Nau's customer-centric style was extended across all channels, including its blog "Thought Kitchen" that pro-moted collective inquiry and its power to affect change on environmental, social, and economic issues. Nau purchased carbon offsets and renewable energy certificates to reduce its carbon footprint in several parts of its business and con-tinued to be an innovative Greentailing leader.

What Nau was bumping up against is asking the consumer to make significant choices in supporting what is undoubtedly a nobly positioned company. The fashions and colors are quite subdued and prices are relatively high because their pursuit of responsibly made clothing adds cost and constrains fashion. While consumers may desire green clothing, will they pay the price? We love the concept but wondered how far it would go, profitably.

Unfortunately, we have our answer, and it may be instructive to every company pursuing green. The basic components of shopping—in this case, fashion and price—must be balanced with eco-needs. We don't see this as an end to green apparel. In the very same day that Nau closed, an article appeared forecasting huge green apparel growth. Nau got too far ahead of itself—a lesson that foreshadows our rules for retail innovation in a later chapter.

Williams-Sonoma, Inc.

Williams-Sonoma, Inc., the specialty retailer of high-quality products for the home, consists of six brands—Williams-Sonoma, Pottery Barn, Pottery Barn Kids, PBteen, West Elm, and Williams-Sonoma Home. Williams-Sonoma, Inc. is one of the largest catalog mailers in the world and in 2006 converted 95 percent of its paper consumption to Forest Stewardship Council (FSC) certified paper. Still, they also remain a voracious mailer of catalogs, and we question how long this can continue before customer response turns negative. While direct marketers and e-commerce purveyors claim they have a "greener" system (no bricks, no trips), there is still inherent waste in their direct-marketing system.

Pottery Barn's spring 2008 catalog was all about "redefining your style" and suggests "It's almost spring! Time to make every room in the home a little greener." The catalog and web site feature a natural green colored background; with products and all the green buzzwords you can think of, like sustainable, organic, recycled, eco-friendly, and natural; and supportive green products by category. The Organic Cotton Collection features cotton that is grown without pesticides or synthetic fertilizers and is sold in colors called fog blue, green haze, and natural. The Green on the Go collection calls to action "Make helping the environment part of your daily routine with our reusable drink bottle and colorful stoneware travel mug" and even "Do-Your-Part" lunch containers.

In the center of the Pottery Barn spring 2008 catalog, the company laid out their "evolving commitment to what's natural." Refreshingly honest and frank, the statement outlines what environmental initiatives the company has taken and what they are committed to doing.

Williams-Sonoma stores introduced their "Pure & Green Collection" of homekeeping soaps, lotions, and cleansers in early 2008. The collection was developed exclusively for Williams-Sonoma by Caldrea and made in the United States and packaged in recycled plastic bottles. Marketed as "A Cleaner Way to Clean," Williams-Sonoma has obviously realized the success found by Method and other "greener" home cleaners and is joining in.

BIG BOX RETAILERS

The Home Depot's Eco Options Program

The Home Depot launched its Eco Options program in April 2007. The Eco Options program is a classification system of products that have less impact on the environment and provides labeling that identifies them as such. The Home Depot initially identified over 2,500 products and has since added more to the program, continuingly working with suppliers in development of new products. Each product offers one or more benefits to sustainable forestry, energy efficiency, healthy home, clean air, and water conservation. When the program started, suppliers were invited to submit their product for consideration to the Eco Options program. Over 60,000 products were submitted, but thousands didn't make the cut. There are currently around 3,000 products in the Eco Options program, organized into five distinct categories:

1. *Sustainable forestry:* featuring green building materials;
2. *Energy efficiency:* with products like the CFL bulb;
3. *Healthy home:* which features more natural and organic cleaning products for around the home;
4. *Clean air:* featuring products that reduce emissions. This could include cleaner lines of paint and specific filters for heating and air-conditioning systems; and
5. *Water conservation:* which features products that reduce water consumption.

The Home Depot began its environmental program on Earth Day of 1990, publishing its Environmental Principles in 1991. The Home Depot is the world's largest home improvement retailer with over 2,100 retail stores in the United States, Puerto Rico, U.S. Virgin Islands, Canada, Mexico, and China and has been a Greentailing innovator with many green retail firsts. It started its green program by using recycled content materials for store and office supplies, advertising, signage, and shopping bags. Early on, it opened a Recycling Depot next to its Duluth, Georgia, store thus becoming the first retail chain to integrate a drive-through recycling center with a store. In 1999, partially in response to consumer watchdog groups, The Home Depot ended its relationship with irresponsible lumber suppliers and became the first in the industry to sell certified wood in partnership with the FSC.

The Home Depot serves as an example of a Greentailer that has taken concrete steps to become more environmentally friendly by incorporating these "principles" into its operations, programs, and customer communications. In the fall of 2007, The Home Depot worked with city and county officials in Atlanta to promote low-flow toilets, showerheads, and other water-saving products, getting local residents involved in the water conservation movement. By localizing its product assortment and being responsive to issues in each store's community, The Home Depot increased its credibility as a socially responsible Greentailer that is sensitive and reactive to its local customer needs.

The tangible connection between the home and conservation is a clear one. It is also clear that consumers need to make trade-off choices constantly in their pursuit of green.

Short-term costs versus long-term benefits; higher cost but more sustainably green products. What is clear in the world of The Home Depot is that the Wal-Mart challenge is not always easy to achieve—saving money and saving the world. Green lumber costs more and is a decision that has no external benefit (you can brag to the neighbors, but you can't see it). Low-flow toilets save water (and costs to the consumer) but may not perform as well. And doesn't everyone like their showers to have full-force pressure?

Conscious consumers will use programs like Eco Options when they are well implemented. Unlike Whole Foods, The Home Depot does not edit choices—it simply points out better options. But while the program is beautifully detailed on the web site, finding eco options in the store is more of a challenge. Signage is limited, and The Home Depot makes it clear that today it is equally concerned about selling what works. Eco options are not a constant on the circular either. The full integration of messaging, from intention to execution, separates out a program versus a sustained method of doing business.

Wal-Mart's Real Green Efforts

There is a wind turbine at the far corner of the parking lot, whirring away on a hot and windy Texas afternoon. The parking lot itself feels and looks different—there is more greenery between the medians and the lot itself gives softly to the touch. Rather than paved with concrete or asphalt, it is porous, allowing rainwater to seep through and be collected in a large retention pool located to the side of the massive building. The stop signs are solar powered and the building itself is framed with open glass with visible solar panels. The inside is also a surprise, with spacious skylights paired with the internal lighting system. When the sun is shining, the fluorescents turn themselves off and the store relies more heavily on natural power.

Is this a futuristic vision of a retail store? No, it's the Wal-Mart Supercenter in McKinney, Texas, one of the initial environmental stores developed by the world's largest retailer. Besides the described elements, there are over 25 active green "experiments" in this store.

If it's not easy being green, it's even harder to be green and Wal-Mart. As the world's largest retailer (and occasionally the world's largest company, including 2007), Wal-Mart is a lightning rod for criticism. Wal-Mart takes heat from just about every conceivable issue from providing health care to associates to providing living wages to its practices with suppliers and sourcing. It is a company with a bulls-eye on its chest (and not just a certain bulls-eye-using competitor bearing down on them) and a poster child for the cause of corporate social responsibility. Yet, when it comes to green, Wal-Mart is out front of many of its retail competitors and not just from a public relations perspective. Wal-Mart has embraced the mission of environmentalism, and it's become a leadership platform for the company.

In CEO and President of Wal-Mart Stores, Inc., Lee Scott's now famous speech, "21st Century Leadership," given in October 2005, Wal-Mart committed to achieving three large sustainability goals: to be supplied 100 percent by renewable energy, to create zero waste, and to sell products that sustain resources and the environment. Through several initiatives, Wal-Mart set out to improve the environment and set in motion a trend that was quickly adopted by other retailers and raised the bar for what it means to be a Greentailer. As the biggest private employer in the United States with over 1.3 million employees and over 4,000 U.S. stores, Wal-Mart's commitment to be a Greentailer has made a significant and tremendous impact.

Wal-Mart's commitment to sustainability extends beyond "Earth-Friendly Products at Budget-Friendly Prices" with strategies implemented in:

- *Land use:* For the Acres for America project, Wal-Mart partnered with the National Fish and Wildlife Foundation on a program to preserve one acre of natural habitat for every acre developed.
- *Supply chain:* Wal-Mart began using a scorecard system in February 2008 that rates its supplier's progress on making product packaging more sustainable. The scorecard evaluates product packaging based on greenhouse gas emissions, product-to-packaging ratio, space utilization, innovation, transportation-related emissions, and the amount of renewable energy used to make the packaging. The program was announced in 2006, and the new scorecard system makes it easy to convey progress toward the goal to trim packaging materials by 5 percent by 2013. Through its energy efficiency programs, Wal-Mart shares best practices in energy efficiency with

suppliers. This idea might be somewhat self-serving, but it also helps the industry to make progress.

• *Packaging:* Working with vendors to increase the use of recycled materials and reducing the packaging size. A recent example is working with its supply community to move toward exclusively concentrated detergents (Ultra) in the laundry category. With Wal-Mart's push, the industry is quickly converting, reducing waste and transportation costs. And Wal-Mart can maximize its space and sell detergents more efficiently. Everyone seemingly wins.

• *Logistics:* With over 7,000 trucks in the United States alone, the Wal-Mart truck fleet is among the largest in the world. Wal-Mart is working with truck manufacturers to increase logistics efficiency through improved truck design and minimizing empty and inefficiently loaded trucks on the road.

• *Energy:* Setting in place more renewable energy sources in manufacturing, storing, packaging, and selling. An example that serves as a visual for Wal-Mart, but a move toward environmental and social responsibility, is the use of CFL bulbs in its operations. By replacing the bulbs in the ceiling fans of all Wal-Mart stores, there is an estimated saving of 47 million annually. And each CFL bulb that consumers purchase saves 30 dollars in purchase prices over the life of the bulb. Wal-Mart announced an ambitious goal of selling 100 million CFL bulbs by the end of 2007. And in typical Wal-Mart fashion, one way to facilitate that was to introduce Great Value CFL bulbs, which drove down the retail costs. Introduced in April 2007, the Live Better Index tracks consumer adoption rates, nationwide and by state, of five sustainable products. CFL bulbs were around a 16 percent national adoption rate and reduced packaging detergent around 22 percent in January 2008. The consumer adoption rate is a percentage based on units sold compared to the entire product category (see Table 5.1).

- *Facilities:* Prototype stores allowed Wal-Mart to develop and test the sustainable practices needed to meet goals. In 2005, Wal-Mart opened two "applied practice" stores in McKinney, Texas, and Aurora, Colorado. More

Table 5.1   Wal-Mart's Live Better Index

	Adoption Rate				
Product	*Nationwide* (%)	*California* (%)	*Illinois* (%)	*Louisiana* (%)	*New York* (%)
Compact fluorescent lights	19.70	23.70	18.50	16.00	23.20
Organic milk	1.58	0.99	0.84	1.83	1.42
Eco-friendly cleaning	4.77	4.1	5.21	3.88	6.02
Organic baby food	4.12	8.58	3.39	3.43	5.21
Extended-life paper products	67.5	73.1	72.3	68.5	54.2
Sustainable coffee	0.35	0.57	0.32	0.12	0.25

Source: Wal-Mart's Live Better Index web site, www.livebetterindex.com (accessed May 6, 2008).

high-efficiency stores have been steadily added and feature:

○ 100 percent integrated water-source format heating, cooling, and refrigeration systems, where water is harnessed to heat and cool the building.

○ LEDs in refrigerator and freezer cases, an estimated 2 to 3 percent energy reduction.

○ Reduction of the use of harsh chemical cleaning products.

○ Daylight Harvesting System uses skylights to refract natural daylight throughout the store and light sensors to monitor available natural light.

• *Climate:* Commitment to reducing total carbon dioxide emissions by 25 percent by 2012. Wal-Mart is the largest private consumer of electricity in the United States and has testified before the U.S. Senate National Resource Committee for strong leadership on climate change. In particular, Wal-Mart supports a mandatory greenhouse gas regulatory system.

In 2007, Wal-Mart opened its first of the High Efficiency, or HE.1 Supercenters in Kansas City. In January 2008, Wal-Mart opened an HE.2 Supercenter in Romeoville, Illinois, that uses new refrigeration and other technologies to improve on the 20 percent energy saving in the HE.1 store (to 25 to 30 percent less energy used compared to a typical store). The latest generation stores use technology tested in the "applied practice" stores and add new conservation measures focused on the refrigeration, water heating, and cooling systems. Where HE.1 was all about publicity and very open green practices, HE.2 is environmentalism in commercial practice—no hype, just a more efficient building (and one of the best-looking Wal-Mart's we've seen).

While it is hard to find fault with Wal-Mart's green efforts (and we do believe that the whole company has embraced the initiative), it does call into question what green really means. While Wal-Mart is addressing the issues of building and altering some of the products it sells, it still must wrestle with how well green rests against the fundamental positioning of the company. For 40 plus years, Wal-Mart has made low prices its single-minded focus. While the shift toward providing a better life is more encompassing, it is questionable whether Wal-Mart can tackle the environment without also tackling the broader issues of Greentailing and addressing at all aspects of what it means to be a socially responsible retailer.

Target

Target has made a commitment to minimizing its environmental footprint through social, environmental, and economic corporate responsibility. The company measures its achievement not just by the bottom line, but also based on its role in the communities each store serves. Since 1946, Target has contributed 5 percent of its annual income to support education, the arts, and social services in local communities.

Target strives to be a responsible steward of the environment through:

- Using resources responsibly;
- Eliminating waste;
- Minimizing its carbon footprint;
- Offering a selection of natural, organic, and eco-friendly products;
- Developing facilities that align environmental, community, and business needs; and
- Influencing vendors and suppliers to embrace sustainable practices.

Target's commitment to waste reduction through its recycling and reuse program cut waste by 70 percent. In 2006, Target recycled or refurbished 47,600 broken shopping carts, 2.1 million pounds of broken plastic hangers, 4.3 million pounds of shrink-wrap from distribution centers, and more than 10,000 pounds of rechargeable batteries.

Target has opened three stores that received Leadership in Energy and Environmental Design (LEED) certification through using less energy, integrating water efficiency, site location, usage of renewable materials, and improved indoor environmental quality. Beginning in 2005, Target has built eight stores in accordance to Low Impact Development (LID), to filter and infiltrate storm-water runoff on site to maintain predevelopment hydrologic conditions. Store features include bio-swales in lieu of storm sewers to manage runoff from parking lots and rain gardens to filter storm water and provide a natural habitat for wildlife.

In existing stores, several measures have been implemented to improve energy efficiency. Target began the process of changing sales floor lighting from a three-lamp to a two-lamp fixture, which will reduce energy consumption by 22 percent. Motion-sensor lighting in stockrooms keep areas lit only when needed. Exterior neon signs at stores are being converted to LED, increasing energy efficiency by 78 percent.

In communicating their values, Target includes facts that point out their commitment to the environment isn't entirely new. For instance, since the early 1990s, Target has used white membranes on store roofs that reflect the sun's heat and helps reduce the heat-island effect of the store.

Endcaps from Gaiam, bamboo mixed linens, and the like have made inroads into their mainstream line-up. As you would expect from Target, its version of the reusable shopping bag is fashionable in comparison to its competitors' versions, but still at a similar price point. Originally developed to comply with laws in California, the fashionable bag was rolled out across the country as demand grew for not only a reusable bag, but also a fashionable one.

Staples

Office supply retailer Staples has made significant strides in recycling and reduction of product packaging. Staples' environmental initiatives are focused around four major cornerstones:

1. Environmentally preferable products,

2. Recycling,

3. Energy and climate, and

4. Environmental education.

Staples eco-modified over 3,000 of its mainstream private-label products to include at least 30 percent postconsumer waste. They have made it easier for customers to recycle by offering a variety of services including consumer electronics and print cartridges. Larger items are recycled for a fee, while smaller items such as computer peripherals are recycled at no charge. Staples reduces energy consumption through the purchase of renewable energy certificates and the installation of on-site renewable energy technologies.

In February 2008, Staples severed all contracts with Singapore-based Asia Pulp & Paper, which accounted for 9 percent of its total paper supply, based on worries that the manufacturer was destroying natural rainforests. Asia Pulp & Paper runs one of Asia's largest pulp mills in Sumatra, and Staples is among several retailers that ended ties with the manufacturer, including Office Depot. Staples has committed to environmental education through partnerships, sponsorships, and their own Staples Foundation for Learning.

Office Depot

Office Depot, a leading retailer of office products and services, publishes their catalog *The Green Book* of environmentally preferable products, in six countries and languages. First tested in 2003, *The Green Book* simplifies the green purchasing experience and was received favorably in the market. It is now issued internationally as well.

The catalog contains thousands of environmentally preferable products and tips and ideas for a "greener office." The actual catalog is printed on 100 percent postconsumer recycled paper with process chlorine-free bleaching, which supports the three main goals in Office Depot's environmental strategy: "increasingly buy green, be green, and sell green."

GROCERY

Whole Foods Market—Greentailing's Poster Child

Whole Foods has to be considered a poster child for all key aspects of the green movement. Its represents the intersection of consumers who have consciously made choices concerning the products they consume and the type of company they choose to do business with. Whole Foods unabashedly makes choices on behalf of the consumer and has taken up causes around product sourcing, safety, and sustainability long before they hit the mainstream presses. The fact that it is growing faster and more profitably than most conventional retailers has grabbed the attention of other retailers. Whole Foods has also drawn the attention, good and bad, of staunch environmentalists who point out inconsistencies in the company's green positioning.

Founded in Austin, Texas, in 1980, Whole Foods differentiates itself from competitors by tailoring its "good for you, good for the environment" product mix to each market, providing a high level of service, high-quality products, and a store environment that is comfortable and easy to shop. Combating the nickname "Whole Paycheck," Whole Foods does command higher prices, but time has proven that consumers are willing to incrementally pay more for quality and green, especially when it is easy. In addition to providing a complete grocery alternative to conventional markets, Whole Foods Market gives its customers a sense of being green through its overall store experience, progressive policies, and from the selling of products themselves. The store is designed to attract quality-oriented customers who are interested in health, nutrition, food safety, and preservation of the environment.

Beyond groceries, Whole Foods has moved into related businesses, such as dietary supplements, personal care products, household goods, and organic cotton apparel. These extensions represent the credibility of the Whole Foods brand and what it means to consumers. The company opened Refresh Spa in December 2006 in the new Whole Foods Market in Dallas, Texas. The 4,500-square-foot spa features all-natural services and products as well as wellness consultations with doctors trained in conventional and alternative medicines.

The company's motto, "Whole Foods, Whole People, Whole Planet" is a key component to not just the messaging but its daily working philosophy. Living and practicing being green is a deep commitment to environmental stewardship that puts the company at the forefront of the effort to make the planet whole and healthy. First and foremost, Whole Foods commitment to green is accomplished through its sourcing and selling of organic products. Organic foods and products are free of synthetic chemical inputs such as pesticides and antibiotics, and since 2002 the U.S. National Organic Program has overseen the use of organic labeling.

Whole Foods is committed to the three Rs: Reduce, Reuse, and Recycle. Among the store's many initiatives, half of its nearly 200 stores participate in a composting program where spoiled produce and waste is hauled to regional facilities. There it is turned into compost and donated to community gardens or sold in stores, reducing landfill waste by up to 75 percent. Whole Foods has also implemented biodegradable food containers for prepared foods.

Beginning in December 2007, the company stopped offering plastic grocery bags at the checkouts in its two stores in Austin, Texas. In early 2008, Whole Foods Market did away with plastic grocery bags in most of its stores and announced that it would eliminate the use of disposable plastic shopping bags by April 22—Earth Day 2008. The 100 percent recycled content paper bags will be the only nonreusable option for shoppers as Whole Foods continues to encourage the use of reusable bags through discount and refund programs. At the Austin stores, the company increased the refund from 5 cents to 10 cents per bag for shoppers who bring their own bags. Whole Foods sells "A Better Bag"—a stylish, reusable bag made from 80 percent postconsumer recycled plastic bottles. The bags sell for 99 cents at checkout areas in all Whole

Foods Market stores nationwide. Many grocery companies are following suit—we have seen green bags popping up all over, from Loblaw's in Canada who has featured them as part of their national advertising to Wegman's, one of our favorite chains in upstate New York.

The company purchased renewable energy credits from wind farms in January 2006 to offset 100 percent of the energy used in its operations, which was the largest wind energy credit purchase on record. Green building innovations are used in newer stores including the use of solar panels, SC certified wood, and recycled steel. In terms of philanthropy, three times a year, 5 percent of net sales go to a local non-profit organization. A majority of these nonprofits have an environmental mission, enhancing Whole Foods credibility as a Greentailer.

Whole Foods Market has been a leading Greentailing innovator, broadening its green impact on other retailers. Whole Foods Market's commitment to local sourcing is one example. After pioneering organics, the company have been on the forefront of going local, defined by actively seeking sourcing closer to its stores. It is also funding start-up farms and small producers to encourage this movement. There is no question that Whole Foods Market is a chain to watch (and emulate) on fronts green and otherwise.

Safeway

Safeway is one of the largest food and drug retailers, operating 1,770 stores in the United States and Canada.

The company communicates its green efforts in an annual environmental initiatives summary report. In tune with current trends, the report summarizes its feeling on green:

> The global consciousness about environmental responsibility continues to awaken.... While the concept of environmental friendliness may seem at odds with maximizing profits, business practices can be modified in numerous ways that benefit both the environment and the bottom line. Safeway has been at the forefront of this consciousness for decades. While we believe in corporate responsibility, we also believe that environmentally friendly business is smart business. Increasingly, consumers are demanding environmental-accountability from suppliers of the goods and services they buy. As we continue to respond to this growing trend, we are branding ourselves as a practitioner of good corporate citizenship while helping sustain the finite resources of the planet we all share.

Safeway is one of the first major U.S. retailers to convert its entire fleet of over 1,000 trucks to cleaner-burning biodiesel fuel.

By converting to biodiesel fuel, an estimated 75 million pounds of carbon dioxide emission will be saved from entering the environment, annually. The biodiesal program is just a slice of Safeway's Greenhouse Gas Reduction Initiative, aimed to address climate change, reduce its carbon footprint, and reduce air pollution. In 2006, Safeway joined the Chicago Climate Exchange (CCX[R]), the world's first and North America's only voluntary, legally binding greenhouse gas emissions reduction, registry, and trading program.

PCC Natural Markets

PCC Natural Markets, with nine locations in the Seattle area, began as a food-buying club of 15 families in 1953. Headquartered in Seattle, PCC Natural Markets is a certified organic retail cooperative with annual sales of $112 million. It is the largest consumer-owned natural foods co-operative in the United States with nearly 40,000 members and thousands more nonmember shoppers. PCC Natural Markets is committed to:

- Advocating high-quality food standards,
- Supporting local, sustainable agriculture,
- Educating consumers about timely issues,
- Operating in an environmentally friendly way, and
- Building community.

PCC, which stands for Puget Consumers Co-Operative, is a full-service grocery of all natural products, meaning that all products are created without synthetic chemicals, additives, or genetically modified ingredients. As a co-op, members are partial owners and store profits go directly back into stores or to the communities it serves. In 2007, the Redmond store location was the first grocery store to qualify for LEED Gold

Certification for exceeding industry standards for energy efficiency and systems performance.

In October 2007, PCC stopped using plastic shopping bags in all store locations (before Whole Foods Market did). According to PCC Natural Markets CEO Tracy Wolpert, "While this decision to eliminate plastic shopping bags will entail some additional cost, it's simply the right thing to do. We have studied the environmental impact of paper versus plastic and believe that paper is the more sustainable choice, while bag reuse is the best choice of all." PCC continues to research other opportunities for incorporating sustainable packaging and supplies.

In early 2008, troubled with current regulations surrounding food ingredient disclosure policies, PCC took a stance with suppliers, requiring full disclosure on all ingredients. Shortly after the January 2008 U.S. Food and Drug Administration ruling that products from cloned animals and their offspring are safe for human consumption, PCC announced that they were in disagreement with the ruling, citing a failure to address several controversial points about animal cloning. As a result, PCC requires all manufacturers to submit a signed agreement that products sold to PCC do not—and will not—contain ingredients from cloned animals or their offspring. PCC CEO Tracy Wolpert said in a press release, "The failure of our regulatory agencies to mandate full disclosure of food ingredients makes it incumbent on leaders in the natural foods industry to step forward and provide what our consumers want. We look forward to working with our trusted suppliers to ensure traceability in the highest quality foods."

Trader Joe's

Trader Joe's, "your neighborhood grocery store" is a discount grocer that offers upscale organic and health foods with over 280 stores in 23 states. Each Trader Joe's—staying true to the "spirit of aloha"—as its store theme, has a local focus in becoming a part of the neighborhood. Each store employs a local artist for in-store signage and supports the local artist community.

Trader Joe's gives back to its local community through donations and involvement in community events. As a testament to its commitment to the neighborhood, each store has its own donations coordinator to focus the store on being a better neighbor. Trader Joe's simple guidelines for requesting donations and involvement in community events are limited to nonprofit organizations such as schools and hospitals. Trader Joe's works with local athletic teams to fight against hunger with programs such as "Trader Joe's Home Runs That Help." For this program, every time the Los Angeles Dodgers hit a home run during a home game, Trader Joe's makes a donation of $250 to the Los Angeles Regional Food Bank.

When in a Trader Joe's, you'll see for sale heavy-duty reusable polypropylene sacks and messaging (local artist drawn) about the benefits of reusing grocery bags. Trader Joe's does a good job of communicating the reasons why reusable bags are good for the customer and the environment.

SUPPLIERS

Method and Cleaner Cleaning Supplies—Eco-Hip

Retailers can't function without suppliers, so it stands to reason that there will be a growing number of suppliers (both new and traditional) rushing to meet the needs of consumers seeking green product. Building green into an integrated differentiation message is far more effective, as Method has been successfully demonstrating.

Method, "People Against Dirty," launched in 2001 as a company with a mission: to revolutionize cleaning. As one of the fastest-growing private companies in the United States, Method has disrupted the cleaning category in formation, packaging, advertising, and merchandising. Founded by Eric Ryan and Adam Lowry in San Francisco, the company "humanifesto" states:

As people against dirty, we look at the world through bright-green colored glasses. We see ingredients that come from plants, not chemical plants, and guinea pigs that are never used as guinea pigs.

Method started with a line of five spray cleaners that were all-natural, biodegradable, and stylishly designed, and gradually added other home cleaning products, from all-purpose cleaners to a laundry care line. As an equal opportunity movement for environment and design (EOMED) member, Method combined design and all-natural function to create a line of products that are more attractive than traditional cleaning products while alleviating the worries of what cleaning toxins might be doing to your home and your body. Available at Target, Safeway stores, Costco, and other mainstream retailers, Method's line of cleaning products aren't difficult to find.

The main challenge for Method is educating the consumer that their products are as effective as traditional cleaning products. In summer 2007, Method launched an advertising campaign called "Detox Your Home," showcasing its biodegradable products. The Method web site's "frequently asked questions" section is full of questions like, "does Method disinfect or kill bacteria?" as well as "is Method safe to use around children?" Marketers have conditioned us to look for actions like antibacterial and ingredients like bleach and ammonia. If we don't see this on the packaging, we question the effectiveness.

But Method is prospering and growing. Although Method only captured 1 percent of the $432 million sales of all-purpose cleaner sales in 2007, year-over-year sales of natural cleaning products rose 23 percent. And, as a result, the traditional cleaning product makers are playing catch-up.

Other examples of all-natural cleaning product companies include Seventh Generation, which captured 0.3 percent of all-purpose cleaning product sales in 2006. Seventh Generation derives its name from the Iroquois belief that "in our every deliberation, we must consider the impact of our decisions on the next seven generations." The company has made a commitment to educating consumers to make more informed choices. They provide consumers the opportunity to make a difference through their purchases by saving natural resources, reducing pollution, and keeping toxic chemicals out of the environment. The company's commitment to educating consumers is demonstrated through its packaging, web site, its *Non-Toxic Times* newsletter, and its brand ambassadors. Topics of the newsletter include the effects of chlorine and petroleum on the environment and comparison of nontoxic cleaners versus traditional household cleaners.

Unilever

Unilever U.S. has saved the equivalent of about 15 million plastic bottles a year by simply reconfiguring the packaging of Suave shampoo to use less plastic. This savings in plastic also represents a huge cost savings for Unilever, one of the world's largest consumer products companies. As a "multilocal multinational" company, Unilever contributes to sustainability in four main ways:

1. Improve people's health through nutrition and hygiene,
2. Minimize its environmental footprint,
3. Secure sustainable supplies of raw materials, and
4. Create wealth and bring benefits to local communities.

Unilever's commitment to sustainability has been a core value of the business for more than a decade. The company produces and updates a sustainable development report to aid in managing social, environmental, and economic impacts.

In October 2005, Unilever introduced All Small & Mighty, a three-times concentrated laundry detergent that is easier to carry, pour, and store. Since its launch, the product has eliminated 10 million pounds of plastic resin, reduced water usage in production by 70 percent compared to the regular size (100 ounce) bottle, cut 81.6 million square feet of paperboard, and saved an estimated 1.4 million gallons of diesel fuel in association with transport costs.

In November 2007, Unilever—in a creative public relations move—started a search for the "Greenest School Kids in America." Unilever unveiled www.gogreenwithall.com, a family-friendly eco-site with tools for parents, kids, and teachers to measure green activities. The winning elementary school received a $50,000 grant toward green improvements like an eco-friendly playground, and every student in the winning school received a green iPod Shuffle with an environmentally friendly solar charger. Like many Greentailers and suppliers, Unilever believes that young students have the passion to help their families become more environmentally active and aware.

Apple

Apple has made a commitment to eliminate toxic chemicals from their new products and to more actively recycle old products. Apple started recycling in 1994 and today operates recycling programs where more than 82 percent of all Macs and iPods are sold. In 2006, Apple recycled 13 million pounds of "e-waste" products and by 2010, the company forecasts it will recycle 19 million pounds. Interestingly, the product's high-quality design and materials are in high demand from recyclers. In this way, Apple products are more sustainable than other computer products.

Examples of Apple eliminating toxic chemicals include past changes and future goals. In 2006, Apple completely eliminated the use of cathode-ray tube (CRT) displays, which contain traces of lead. Apple plans to completely eliminate the use of arsenic in all of its displays by the end of 2008 and reduce and eventually eliminate the use of mercury by transitioning to LED backlighting. Apple is constantly refining its product design to maximize efficiency while minimizing waste. Apple follows the requirements of programs such as ENERGY STAR®.

GREENER OUTDOORS

Timberland

Timberland is an outdoor apparel specialty retailer with a mission to "equip people to make a difference in their world." Timberland employees who purchase hybrid vehicles are rewarded with preferential parking and a $3,000 credit toward the car's purchase price. Timberland also encourages reusable shopping bags. Timberland has introduced reusable bags, called "Trash Is My Bag" totes, made from recycled plastic bottles that sell for $5.50 each or come free with a $100 purchase.

Timberland operates www.timberlandserve.com, which outlines the company's commitment to corporate social responsibility through environmental stewardship, global labor standards, and community involvement.

REI

REI operates over 80 outdoor specialty stores in 27 states and has been at the forefront of green building. REI has been recognized as one of the "100 Best Companies to Work For" in the United States by *Fortune* magazine every year since 1998. REI offers generous perks and flexible benefits programs (for full-and part-time employees) that foster a healthy work culture.

In 2004, the REI Portland, Oregon store became the first retail store in the country to earn LEED-Commercial Interior (CI) Gold certification and in 2006, the Pittsburgh store earned LEED-CI Silver certification. But even before the LEED certification program existed, REI was incorporating green design elements such as natural lighting and better air quality into all its stores.

Nike

Like many publicly traded companies, Nike issues a corporate responsibility report that outlines what it is doing to benefit society. Nike follows a "considered design ethos" across all its footwear lines that combines premium design and performance with environmental sustainability. By 2011, Nike pledges that all its footwear will meet or exceed its sustainability standards; by 2015, all its apparel; and by 2020, all its equipment. The company's sustainability standards call for 17 percent reduction in waste, 30 percent reduction in packaging and point of purchase waste, and that all Nike brand facilities and business travel will be climate neutral.

Nike launched its sustainable product time—the Considered Line—and has committed to sourcing as much of the products' raw materials as possible—recycled polyester and rubber, organic cotton, hemp—from within 200 miles of where it is produced, cutting the environmental and financial costs of transportation. Keep in mind that the Considered line is made in China and Thailand, so the cost of transport to the end consumer isn't calculated into the agenda.

Gaiam

Gaiam was founded in Boulder, Colorado, in 1988 as a provider of information, goods, and services to customers who value the environment, a sustainable economy, healthy lifestyles, alternative health care, and personal development. Part of the company's mission, as listed on the Gaiam web site, says that "Gaiam was founded to make a difference in the world by educating people about lifestyle choices that affect personal development, wellness, and environmental responsibility."

The core of Gaiam is environmental and social responsibility and so it comes as no surprise that its green efforts are fully integrated in everything it does. Gaiam even encourages customers to request limiting the number of catalogs they send and to instead shop the web site, where all products are featured, allowing customers to stop receiving catalogs entirely. Gaiam products are now showing up at Target as well, suggesting its customer base is expanding.

GREENER BUILDINGS

Green Exchange

Green Exchange, located in Chicago, is the country's first business community dedicated to environmental sustainability, profit, and positive social impact. The 272,000-square-foot loft building, a potential LEED certified platinum renovation, will be home to more than 100 like-minded businesses purveying a variety of green products and services. The mission of Green Exchange is to foster success within the green business economy by helping to move the green marketplace from niche to mainstream while serving people, planet, and profit.

Chicago-based Baum Development, located no more than a few miles from Green Exchange, is a real estate development company specializing in the acquisition and redevelopment of underutilized properties. In September 2005, the Baum brothers, who own and manage the company, purchased the 93-year-old former lamp factory building. The Baums wanted to develop the building with a triple bottom-line approach that would not only provide a financial return but also give back to the community and promote environmental sustainability. However, it wasn't until they were approached by Barry Bursak, a Chicago resident and long-time proponent of bringing green alternatives to the marketplace, that the idea for Green Exchange was born. The concept was rich with possibility, and the timing was right to create an entirely green business community, housed in a green building to serve the needs of a burgeoning green customer base in the Chicago area.

The amenities of Green Exchange have mass appeal; however tenancy is limited to green businesses. According to co-owner David Baum, a tenant must embrace eco-friendly, fair trade, and/or socially responsible practices in order to lease space. The building will feature a 60,000-gallon cistern on the ground floor to store rainwater to irrigate plants and grasses on the green roof. The building also has an escalator that uses 30 percent less energy than traditional escalators because it is designed to monitor the total weight of the passengers at any given time and adjust its power draw accordingly. The fewer the people on the escalator, the less power needed. Tenants will enjoy cleaner air as a result of nontoxic construction materials and coatings and better ventilation.

Located near the Kennedy Expressway, Green Exchange is easily accessible via the Chicago Transit Authority bus system, encouraging the use of public transportation. To accommodate all tenants, the building features a garage with priority parking for hybrids and outlets to recharge electric vehicles, as well as indoor bike storage rooms.

In addition to the criteria set for LEED certification buildings, Green Exchange has other amenities that are meant to cultivate green innovation and build a green community. The building has 57 work/live units ranging from 700 to 1,500 square feet. These lofts are designed for use by green business owners who want kitchenette and bath amenities in their office space or for those who chose to live in their workspace. According to Phil Baugh, director of leasing for the Green Exchange, the building "will be a think tank or business incubator. Tenants will be able to share best practices and advance their sustainability learning curve exponentially compared to if they were in an isolated storefront." In addition to the benefits of proximity to other green businesses, tenants will also be able to share a common customer pool and increase their exposure to consumers interested in purchasing green products and services.

Green Exchange has gained national attention and local government support. Chicago Mayor Richard M. Daley wants "Chicago to be a shining example of how a major urban area can live in harmony with its environment. Green Exchange is a great example of the public/private partnerships that are working together to help make Chicago one of the most environmentally friendly cities in the nation." With a broad mix of tenants, initial green businesses include a wholesale and retail green building supply company, energy consultants, an ecological printer, and a green pet-supply store.

Clearly, though early in the development cycle, Greentailing is moving from concept to practice. The broad range of activities being carved out by retailers and suppliers alike demonstrates the traction that Greentailing has. Undoubtedly, by the time this book hits the press, there will be many new and even better Greentailing ideas being implemented.

CHAPTER SIX

Putting Green Practices into Action

Green is not a trend, it's a new way of life for us.
Going green is not going to go away.[1]
> —*Dan Butler, NRF Vice President of*
> *Merchandising and Retail Operations*

A t the National Retail Federation (NRF) annual convention and expo in January 2008, the Green Pavilion exhibit showcased environmental products and solutions and offered information on how retailers can be environmentally conscious while still contributing to their bottom line. The Green Pavilion served as a platform for new product launches like IBM's Green Retail Store of technologies and services that were created to improve energy and operational efficiency in a retailer's information technology systems. Other items on display included recycled plastic gift cards and kiosks made from organic waste material. At the convention, Wal-Mart, Kohl's, Best Buy, L.L. Bean, among other retailers made presentations about their green efforts and how these efforts have proven fruitful. NRF president and CEO, Tracy Mullin, said, "As the retail landscape becomes more competitive, the idea of conserving energy and resources becomes more important—not only to gain customers' trust but also to improve the bottom line."

This view is supported by Wal-Mart's green efforts, which kicked off in 2005, at a time when Wal-Mart was (and remains) on the hot seat for its labor and health-care practices. Leslie Dach, Wal-Mart's executive vice president of corporate affairs and government relations, believes every little change can mean a big cost savings. As an example, an employee suggested turning off the lights in the breakroom vending machines. By removing the vending machine lightbulbs in all the breakroom vending machines companywide, they save an estimated $1 million a year in electricity (the joys of being a $350 billion corporation!).

The retail sector has a unique and powerful position linking production and consumption. Because of this, retail plays an important and influential role in the context of the environment and sustainability. As consumer demand for environmental responsibility becomes increasingly apparent, retailers are making changes, large and small, to meet or beat green expectations. The goal for any Greentailer is to strive for more sustainable operations, educate suppliers and consumers on how to become greener, and to not adversely impact their bottom line or significantly disrupt current operations.

For green efforts to be a success, they must be measurable and they must be incorporated in all aspects of business, not just in messaging (or greenwashing). What kick-started some retailers into going green was the increased awareness that green isn't just a public relations necessity but can be profitable as well.

The most important aspect of putting green into action is getting started. It take years to develop fully integrated and comprehensive programs and perhaps decades to truly change, cycling through old practices, inefficient and outdated buildings, and entrenched consumer habits. We've looked closely at Greentailers and identified four key techniques for going green—thinking green, acting green, selling green, and conveying green.

THINKING GREEN

Incorporate Green Initiatives into Your Mission and Core Values

As a fundamental tenant of any business, outlining green initiatives should start with a company's mission and be included as a part of the core values. The organization then understands the commitment to being environmentally and socially responsible and sets an ambitious mandate. Without a defined goal, green initiatives may be well-intentioned but lack any real purpose. Setting goals concerning waste reduction, building efficiency, and commitment to a percentage of green products helps galvanize the organization.

Develop Green Advocates within Your Organization

At large companies, this means the appointment of a chief green officer or someone in upper management who has direct responsibility for managing green initiatives. At most companies, this becomes the role of the owner/operator or a committed individual. Better still is the formation of a green committee to review and change practices within the company. Because green is comprehensive, it needs multiple looks and multiple touches to align aspects of real estate, merchandising, operations, procurement, and other functions. It won't happen, however, if there isn't a mandate. In a similar way, retailers need to get suppliers involved early. Best-practice sharing is a highly effective way to learn and find quick wins.

Good green suggestions should come from everywhere in the organization. Creating both internal and external communication forums will enable ideas to incubate. While most retailers are not likely to save $1 million on vending machine lights like Wal-Mart, there are hundreds of ways to reduce, recycle, and reuse that can be implemented on a grassroots basis. It also helps give advocates a forum.

ACTING GREEN

Design Environmentally and Energy Efficient Buildings

The Leadership in Energy and Environmental Design (LEED) Green Building Rating System, developed by the

U.S. Green Building Council (USGBC), provides standards for environmentally sustainable construction and is a nationally accepted benchmark for green buildings. Since its inception, LEED has certified over 14,000 projects in the United States. Retailers can benefit from the over 70 regional USGBC chapters nationwide providing green building resources and education. The LEED certification guidelines aid in ensuring that buildings meet the requirements set forth in the five key areas: sustainable site development, water savings, energy efficiency, materials selection, and indoor environmental quality.[2] Some of the benefits of a LEED certified building include:

- Lower operating costs and increased asset value
- Conservation of energy and water
- Healthier and safer environment for occupants
- Reduction of greenhouse gas emissions
- Possible qualification for tax rebates, zoning allowances, and other incentives
- Commitment to environmental stewardship and social responsibility

LEED certification is possible for both new and existing buildings. Many projects are achieving LEED certification within their budgets and in the same cost range as non-LEED projects. Even without LEED certification, there are some proven design features that are incorporated into newer buildings. The use of skylights to reduce lighting costs, fluorescent lighting systems for commercial use, and LED lighting in freezer cases are just a few examples. It doesn't hurt to publicize your efforts. Tesco's Fresh & Easy stores utilize their endcaps to promote their environmental friendliness, from energy conscious fleets to reusing all display materials.

Develop Efficient Methods for Dealing with Waste

Packaging constitutes the largest component of waste at retail stores. By working with supplier and vendors, it is possible to reduce or even eliminate excess packaging for products coming into the store. Environmentally friendly packaging options are now more affordable, and replacing plastic clamshell packaging with paperboard-blister hybrid packaging is a simple and cost effective way to be green. When possible, packaging can be reused through recycling or donation.

A growing trend in office supply and consumer electronics retailers, among others is recycling and trade-in programs for PCs and other, often obsolete, electronic equipment. Costco warehouse stores partnered with GreenSight, a global supply chain solutions provider, for a recycling and trade-in program offered for free to its members. The recycling program employs a zero tolerance landfill policy, meaning everything possible is reused, and GreenSight and Costco both benefit from sales of refurbished equipment and recycled products. Mobile phone retailers are also participating through recycling services for old phone equipment and batteries.

Promote Eco-Friendly Packaging

One of the easiest and most visible ways to show commitment to green is offering for sale reusable shopping bags as an alternative to disposable paper and plastic bags. In early 2008, Whole Foods Market did away with plastic grocery bags in most of its stores and eliminated the usage of disposable plastic shopping bags on Earth Day, April 22, 2008. Walgreens, Safeway stores, Trader Joe's, Target, and Wal-Mart, to name just a few, sell reusable bags as an alternative to plastic bags. According to Swedish furniture giant Ikea, the average American family of four throws away about 1,500 bags a year, and less than 1 percent of bags are recycled.[3] In March 2007, Ikea began charging 5 cents for each disposable plastic bag, cutting usage in half (and, as you'd expect, selling reusable bags).

Creating incentives for customers to reuse bags helps fuel the cause, such as a savings off a customer's purchase. While reducing plastic bags is impactful, other forms of packaging need to be addressed to ensure that wasteful practices are curtailed. The best part of these initiatives is a win-win for the company—saving the environment and saving costs.

Convert to Energy-Conscious Fleets

With gas prices at all time highs, increasing fuel efficiency of truck fleets can result in significant cost savings. Wal-Mart has one of the largest private trucking fleets in the world, and they plan to double new truck efficiency by 2015. As stated on the company's web site, Wal-Mart believes "that these investments and innovations will spark industry-wide changes in vehicle platform, engine and transportation efficiencies, create jobs, reduce foreign oil dependency, and increase the quality of life for our stakeholders. Overall, these commitments will reduce our footprint and buy us much-needed time for everyone to transition to a more sustainable future." Some of the innovative elements of the new generation of trucks include trailer side skirts that reduce wind resistance, super single tires that better fuel economy, aerodynamic tractor packages that reduce the fuel required to operate the truck, reduced weight tag axles, and an auxiliary power unit that eliminates the use of the main engine for warming the cabin. In January 2008, Safeway announced that it is the first major retailer to make its entire fleet of trucks operate on biodiesel fuels. We are sure more will follow, especially since saving costs, in this case, also saves the environment.

Offset Carbon Emissions

Many retailers are using *carbon offsets* to achieve the status of being "carbon neutral." So what does that mean exactly? Through purchasing carbon offsets, which are basically credits for emission reductions achieved through other projects, you can counterbalance your own polluting emissions. Wind farms, solar installations, or other energy efficient projects are common sources for emission reduction credits.

Retailers can use web-based carbon footprint calculators to determine their energy use and greenhouse emissions.

Carbon offsets offer the flexibility of choosing how many emissions to offset. In January 2006, Whole Foods Market purchased renewable energy credits from wind farms to offset 100 percent of the electricity used in all stores, facilities, bakehouses, distribution centers, regional offices, and national headquarters in the United States and Canada. This represented the largest wind energy credit purchase ever in the United States.

Get Involved

Policies are now being set and standards created for a new era of Greentailing. This includes laws about plastic bag use, labeling standards for products, initiatives for cleaner air, water and waste reduction, and so on. Leading retailers have the opportunity, and almost an ultimatum, to become active participants in shaping the next generation of green.

SELLING GREEN

Source and Promote Products That Are Environmentally Responsible

Green retail concepts are rapidly being developed but aren't likely to dominate the retail landscape. Customers will continue to shop at their regular outlets, and these retailers need to be incorporating environmentally friendly products into their stores. For apparel retailers, it might mean creating lines of organically made clothing. For supermarkets, it often means featuring green based cleaning supplies and promoting organic or sustainable products. At home stores, it could be carrying products that help consumers with energy conservation. And so on down the line.

Physical retail stores are just the tip of the iceberg for green. Working with suppliers to create more efficient products and reduce supply chain costs represents a huge opportunity. Selling local products could lead to reduced delivery costs, but it also communicates a support for the community and provides for a more personalized store experience.

CONVEYING GREEN

Corporate Social Responsibility

CSR involves a never-ending list of interests and actions where a company takes responsibility for its impact on all the stakeholders. CSR reports, commonly published alongside company annual reports, are an opportunity to publicly convey commitment to green. All stakeholders get the message. CSR reports help communicate a company's core values and beliefs and update stakeholders on progress toward goals.

Green Communication Systems

In addition to a CSR report, creating a green communications system is one way to help consumers understand a company's commitment to green and help them feel like a more responsible consumer. Office Depot has a green-friendly catalog. The Home Depot launched the Eco Options Program in April 2007 as a method to communicate its over 2,500 products that have less of an impact on the environment. Publix Super Markets has an overarching program (and pilot stores) called Greenwise that helps consumers easily identify eco-friendly products. Most retailers, however, won't be a Whole Foods, who create a store around green. Consumers need clear programs and communications to help them understand green options and to provide shortcuts for identifying green items.

Encourage Transparent Policies

One fact that cannot be overlooked is that consumers have changed. Consumers have the ability to access information like never before. They are savvy researchers at finding out what is important to them. Retailers need to be as transparent as possible in regards to policies of CSR. It will be critical to have strong policies and CSR in competing for a more enlightened workforce and for attracting customers who will place more importance on socially responsible values in the future.

Be Charitable

Giving back to the community in ways that are unique and connected with the business's vision is a great way to convey commitment to green, as well as providing an opportunity to connect with groups in community. We've seen several examples we like, and sometimes the simpler the idea the better. Starting a company sponsored program or charity is a great way to draw attention to greenness.

SUMMARY

Greentailers' customers feel responsible buying from Greentailers that are committed to reducing their impact on the environment, providing their employees with an improved working environment. Greentailers have increased their goodwill, saved money, and reduced waste.

Successful Greentailers:

- *Think green:* They create clear and credible green aspirations that align with the core business strategy and establish trust.
- *Act green:* They formulate ways to construct the whole organization around green aspirations and maintain green credibility with all groups.
- *Sell green:* They sell green products and services wholly or as an alternative to nongreen products.
- *Convey green:* They are responsible corporate citizens and communicate this by giving back to the community in ways that are unique and connected with the business's vision.

When looked at in combination, Greentailers represent a radical change in every aspect of business policy, causing a massive inflection point.

CHAPTER SEVEN

THE HOT FIVE—OTHER REVOLUTIONARY THEMES IN RETAIL

A t this point, we are up to our eyeballs in green. While there is no question that retailers and suppliers are going to be rapidly changing many of their business practices to become greener, it also very likely that only a small percent will orient their entire business toward green. The fundamentals of retail success remain the same— finding the right mix of product, price, service, and location that appeals to a particular set of target customers. While the world is getting greener and green needs to be an element of future business strategy, it is clearly not the only element.

We still need to answer the question: "What's Next?" What other ideas have the potential to create a revolution in retailing? And just as importantly, what constitutes a retail revolution?

A retail revolution represents an actual manifestation of an inflection point. A profound shift in the way business is done. With a quick look back at the history of retailing, some obvious points jump out. Here's a quick list of 10 revolutions that greatly impacted retailing's immediate past:

1. Marshall Field's (and others) in the development of the modern day department store, amassing an array of goods into a single point of distribution.

2. Sears, Roebuck and Montgomery Ward and the development of direct retailing, allowing goods to be available to customers in remote locations.

3. Piggly Wiggly, A&P, King Kullen, and others for the development of the self-service supermarket, allowing for lower-priced groceries and expanded assortments.

4. Kresge (Kmart) and the development of the modern day discount store, which reduced service (sorry, Mr. Field), simplified operations, and created a lower-priced model.

5. Toys"R"Us and the development of the modern day category killer model, expanding range in a focused category and providing greater assortments than general merchandisers (sorry, again, Marshall Field's and Sears).

6. Ray Kroc and McDonald's, for creating fast, cheap, and consistent foods to go, liberating the American housewife from the kitchen.

7. Les Wexner and The Limited and the development of specialized apparel stores targeting a specific set of customers for specific occasion needs.

8. Price Club and the development of the membership warehouse club, reinventing the business model, drastically take costs out of the system by limiting range and focusing fanatically on productivity.

9. Wal-Mart and the adaptation of the European hypermarket into the U.S. Supercenter, offering incredible range and prices under one roof and creating the most formidable (and successful) retail format of all time.

10. Amazon.com and the development of e-commerce, providing virtual commerce and changing forever our notions of selection and information.

Each of these revolutions changed the nature of business, spawned a raft of imitators, and contributed to the shortening of the life cycle of their predecessors. And as was often the case, each was viewed with a healthy dose of skepticism as they first made their appearance—the inflection point was recognized after the fact.

Many of these revolutions have happened relatively recently, and there are many candidates for new revolutions currently in the works. Will it be Whole Foods, for ushering in an era of Greentailing? Perhaps Aldi, for its expanding notion of extreme discounting? Will it be Zara or H&M, European imports who created the notion of fast fashion, changing the fashion cycle and shaking up traditional notions of speed in retail? Maybe it's Apple or Coach, who are mastering direct relationships with customers? Who will finally fully nail multichannel retailing in all of its aspects? The race for what's next, for developing the next big thing, is a constant endeavor in retailing, and the winner can become very successful indeed.

As we scan the retail landscape, it is clear that there is a rich tapestry of retail formats that are enjoying success. One of the main principles of our -Est model was to describe a world of retail success that wasn't simply black (price) or white (service). (In our first book, *Winning at Retail: Developing a Sustained Model for Retail Success,* we discussed in depth what we call our -Est model, which recognizes that in order to win in retail you have to develop a clear point of view and dominate an attribute, such as price or service, that your target customer really desires). Too often, retail is viewed in a simple one-dimensional matrix—the reality is far more complicated. What we can agree on is that the obvious range of consumer needs are now being met, and by and large being met well. There is more retail space than ever before and the quality of retailers servicing that space has grown steadily better. Where we once witnessed a universe of pretty good retailers serving the customer's needs, we are now finding that just the best are surviving, with the others being ruthlessly weeded away, condemned to the black hole of retail oblivion.

It seems like a daunting task to discover new niches in the marketplace. Entrenched competitors typically have better resources, real estate, buying power, systems, and procedures, and a host of other built-in advantages. Most importantly, they already have customers coming to their stores. But, for the very same reason, they are also often at a disadvantage in attempting to create real change. They become entrenched in a single way of doing things, and changing systems, procedures, merchandise, and culture can be extraordinarily difficult. And they have a lot to lose—namely those existing customers and their loyalty. We have long heard the lament that there are no good ideas left. Yet, we also see new ideas constantly and new retailers enjoying huge success.

While there is no easy formula for new retailing success, we have looked at enough successes and failures to develop some basic principles.

THE HOT ZONE

Tomorrow's hot ideas are predictable if retailers pay attention to the right trends. The key to realizing and developing a hot idea is to correctly assess three things: the needs of customers, the competitive environment, and the retailer's own internal strengths and weaknesses.

What we call the *Hot Zone* is where many of tomorrow's most successful ideas come from. It lies at the intersection of correctly responding to consumer trends, determining a retailer's capability of delivering on a strategy, and finding a defendable market position versus competition.

Consider Target, the self-proclaimed "upscale discounter." Target tapped into a consumer trend by realizing that even wealthy and middle-income shoppers would flock to discount stores. And rather than selling dowdy (and cheaper) products, which was the staple of most discounters, Target decided to sell these customers trend-right, fashion-forward merchandise. Target was able to accomplish this extraordinary merchandising feat because it leveraged heavily from the internal strengths of its parent company, which operated high-fashion department stores. Target's culture understood and embraced fashion. Finally, Target hit a defensible market position because Wal-Mart and Kmart were content to attract customers with low prices, opting for inexpensive goods rather than fashionable merchandise. Target hit the bull's-eye of the Hot Zone. And, not surprisingly, it has become a spectacularly successful retailer, even as it directly faced off against of the most extraordinarily successful and formidable retailer in history, Wal-Mart.

But coming up with the concept for a hot idea is just the beginning. For a hot idea to succeed, a store must simultaneously meet consumer needs, be easily understood, and be operated profitably. Achieving this is the great challenge—and the great thrill—of creating a new retail concept.

A winning concept requires retailers to be diligent students of consumer trends. It also requires them to start with consumers: How do they behave now? Why? How will they behave in the future? Why? How does this concept benefit specific customers? To become a hot idea, a new concept must first solve a real problem for consumers. Are there enough consumers out there in a defined trade area of the market to support the new proposition? Too many new concepts are conceived to solve problems for the retailers—to foster growth or expand a fast-growing division or one that is the CEO's pet-project. Too many ideas are launched that overestimate the real size of the market. In many ways, we fear that is a challenge that many green retail concepts face today.

After determining how the new concept helps consumers, the retailer has to figure out how to communicate the concept's proposition. Great concepts (-Est concepts) are easily understood because they are built on a compelling proposition. Far too often, we see new concepts that try to straddle lots of potentially intriguing ideas but succeed at none. If someone says, it's like Starbucks meets Ben & Jerry's—watch out. There's a reason why the best ice cream positioning and the best coffee proposition are mutually exclusive. The black hole is never very far behind.

Yet, one of the hotter ideas, with lines around the block, is Pinkberry—the best frozen yogurt, twenty-first century style. And we're seeing some success (although at times a bit of head scratching) with cream puff stores (Beard Papa) and cupcake stores. Simple propositions make lots of sense to customers—just make sure the niche is big enough.

Last, the retailer must figure out how to deliver on that proposition with acceptable profits. Developing an acceptable economic model is always harder than it appears. It takes years and many prototypes to develop the right size, the right labor mix, the right merchandise assortments, the right amount to spend on construction and build out, the right message to the consumer, and so on. Far too often, new retail concepts are shelved because the parent company ran out of time, money, or patience (and sometimes all three). We have participated in some new concept start-ups that faced this challenge—we were convinced that the key to the concept finally making it was just around the corner as the plug was being pulled.

In the chapters that follow, we break out some of the most fertile ground for hot ideas that can fuel the next revolution. We have identified five areas, driven by demography, consumer behavior, or responses to the competitive marketplace, as follows:

1. Demographic Shifts Provide Retail Opportunities;

2. Moving Up the Ladder—Growth of Experiential Retailing—How to Drive Sales and Profits Beyond Price;

3. Getting Outside the Box—New Ways to Reach the Consumer—The Growth of Non-store Retailing;

4. Selling Services, Not Just Products; and

5. Brands Going Retail—The Battle for Control of the Customer.

For each of these areas, we detail the reasons for the trend and profile some retail companies who exemplify the concept.

What's going to have the greatest impact on the future? While not clear, we do know that retail will continue to change dramatically in the future. A more demanding customer, access to capital and a shortening retail life cycle guarantee it.

CHAPTER EIGHT

DEMOGRAPHIC SHIFTS PROVIDE RETAIL OPPORTUNITIES

D emographics are powerful predictors of consumer behavior. Age, income, education, sex, ethnicity, household composition, and occupation are the classic metrics demographers use to document the "numbers" of our society. Retailers talk about demographics a lot and use them as part of their target customer profiles, but our experience has been that few retailers have really capitalized on them. The shifts in demographics over the past 25 years have created significant changes in the ways consumers behave in retail settings (particularly how and where they shop and what they buy) and, as a result, huge opportunities exist for retailers to find winning "white spaces." (*Note:* "White spaces" are places that provide opportunities to meet consumers' unfilled needs.)

A LOOK AT U.S. DEMOGRAPHIC TRENDS

In Chapter Two, we discussed some of the big demographic trends. They are hardly surprises:

- The population is clearly aging and that has created extremely demanding consumers who know their likes and dislikes, and whose bodies, personal, as well as family needs have changed.

- The makeup of the U.S. household is clearly different today that 25 years ago. No more Ozzie-and-Harriet households, or at least there are no more of them than single households with children headed by female (both around 12 percent of the roughly 110 million households in the United States). The big drivers of this change are working women (roughly 75 percent of women are in the workforce today) and the fact that in 2007 more households are unmarried than married.

- The ethnic population is exploding, particularly among Hispanic and Asian populations, which is having a powerful influence on fashion, food, and entertainment. Given current trends, Caucasians will no longer represent the majority of the U.S. population.

- A significant polarization of income and wealth has separated the haves from the have-nots. Only the top echelons of society have had any increase in real income over the past 25 years (after inflation). The rest of society is struggling to live on a tight budget.

Most discussions on demographics also focus on the "generations." Every demographer seems to have a slightly different definition for them, but most include the criteria in Table 8.1.

Given the year a person is born (and subsequently the periods he or she moves through and experiences the various stages of life) determines his or her generational label. And the implications are that everyone with the same label, thinks and acts the same way, and has the same set of values. There is considerable truth to this and, many retailers have capitalized and are continuing to capitalize on it.

Capitalizing on Future Demographic Shifts

Much of the power of demographics as it relates to shopping behavior, retail formats, and even retailing revolutions centers on life stage and household composition. Life stages are fairly well defined—infant, childhood, tweens, teens, young

Table 8.1   Generations

Name	Definition
Depression	Born in 1932 or before. In 2007, members are 75-years-old or older.
World War II	Born between 1933 and 1945. In 2007, members are between the ages of 62 and 74.
Baby boomers	Born between 1946 and 1964. In 2007, members are between the ages of 43 and 61.
Generation X (Gen X)	Born between 1965 and 1976. In 2007, members are between the ages of 31 and 42.
Boomlets (Gen Y)	Born between 1977 and 1994. In 2007, members are between the ages of 13 and 30.
Post-Millenniums	Born from 1994 to present. In 2007, members are 12-years-old or younger.

adult, household/family formation, household with young children, household with older children, empty nesters, grandparents, active retirement, inactive retirement, and so on. If you know where an individual is on the life-stage ladder, and have insight into their household income and sex, you are well armed with the most powerful predictors of shopping behavior: who and how that person shops and what and where they buy. And good retailers have recognized that targeting life-stage directly with a retail format or concept has considerable chance of success, particularly if it meets their unfilled needs.

An even sharper focus on demographics provides additional opportunity for the retailing revolution. As generations move into new life stages, innovative retailers are developing formats and concepts that are just right for smaller and smaller demographic segments.

Getting to Where the Puck Is Going to Be . . . Ahead of the Big Demographic Shifts

Two important facts about demographics: They change slowly and they are fairly predictable. Demographically, the vision of the future three to five years out is quite clear. As an example, the classic age wave of the various generations (based on 2005 U.S. Census Bureau data) is shown in Figure 8.1. As we age and live longer, the wave keeps moving to the right.

The secret to success in retail development, as we mentioned earlier, is getting ahead of the puck (wave in this case)—developing an idea or format or concept that is just

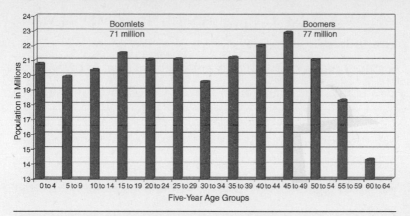

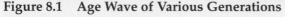

Figure 8.1   Age Wave of Various Generations

Source: McMillan|Doolittle, 2007. U.S. Census Bureau.

right for a large enough target segment or generation as they move into a new life stage.

Focusing on Baby Boomers as They Move into Their Next Life Stage

Baby boomers have been one of the most important demographic generations in U.S. history and they will continue to be in the future. We don't know what to call their next life stage, as more and more baby boomers move into empty nests and eventual retirement (it won't be retirement in the classical sense because baby boomers have changed every previous life stage they have passed through). But we do know baby boomers' wants and needs will be different than the generations that preceded them, that the market is not clearly understood today, and that the potential will be significant, particularly in retail services. The size of the opportunity: over $2.1 trillion in spending power in 2006, which is 16 times that of Generation X and 12 times that of Generation Y.

Yet, these baby boomers have not been easy to categorize; and stores for "old people" haven't cut it to date. More to the point, there will be a huge demand for products and services for people who steadfastly don't want to be old. There will be explosive growth in beauty treatments of all sorts and gigantic growth in the skin-care market. Foods that make you feel younger and fitter will boom. Clothing and accessories that complement an aging boomer's body will resonate . . . and so on.

At the same time, there will also be significant real needs. Pharmaceutical products have experienced near double-digit compound growth. Products that make you see better, hear better, look better will grow. And there needs to be some practical changes happening in retail stores as well. Better lighting, lower aisles, bolder print on signage, smaller stores with less congestion all represent subtle changes to accommodate the aging baby boomers. Little hints are popping up here and there, like magnifying glasses in the aisle at your favorite drugstore and point sizes on type getting subtly larger.

The baby boomer will not age easily and will represent gigantic opportunities for companies who get it early and get it right.

Who's Getting It Right with Aging Baby Boomers?

- *Publix Super Markets:* The incredibly successful Florida supermarket chain does the basics very well—wide aisles, no clutter, no items out of place, large print pricing and labels. And there is legendary customer service to boot. This earned them a prominent feature as an Easiest retailer in our first book. Like any great retailer, Publix continues to evolve and grow. Publix, with a concentration of stores in communities with older demographics, is also on top of the key trends that matter more to the baby boomer trade. Consider some of their more recent efforts. They have developed a program called Apron's, which began as a cooking school in some of their larger stores. Now, the Apron's brand is being put to work throughout the store. There are Apron's cooking demo centers in many of their stores, offering helpful hints to putting a meal on the table fast. And there is Apron's catering and party planning—boomers do lots of entertaining at home. Or, how about the Apron's meal assembly services, where you can fix a week's worth of meals in one sitting. This copies chains like Dream Dinners and Dinners By Design, but Publix has the credibility and products to pull it off. Publix has also launched another integrated brand—Greenwise. Greenwise began as the designation for natural and organic products within their stores. It has products under its name and also serves as the header throughout the store (produce, meat, grocery) to identify healthier products. Clearly, health and wellness is its own mega-trend fueled by baby boomers. Greenwise also became a test store, with Publix competing more directly against Whole Foods.

- *Coldwater Creek:* Apparel stores for aging baby boomers need to walk a very fine line. How do you balance the obvious needs of older customers without sacrificing their desire to look and feel young and fashionable? No easy trick and brands routinely identify their target customers to be significantly younger than they really are. There are lots of "youth-chasing" retailers in the mall, and maybe, coincidentally, a reason why so many apparel retailers are struggling. Coldwater Creek apologizes less for its positioning than most—bright, colorful clothing for an older consumer. They are having some bumps along the road, but they have transitioned successfully from a direct marketing to a multichannel retailer with huge store growth planned ahead for a demographic with money to spend and relatively few options.

- *Oops—Forth & Towne:* When Gap announced plans for a new chain focused on an older woman boomer, it was met with initial optimism, given the facts and trends about the woman boomer. But, they were forced to close Forth & Towne after only being open for 18 months. Why? For one, the troubles at Gap, Inc. were bigger than a new format would solve. More importantly, Forth & Towne probably suffered most from overambition. Rather than roll out one brand, the store simultaneously introduced four (Prize, Allegory, Gap Edition, and Vocabulary) geared for different needs in a woman's life. Its competitors (Chico's and Coldwater Creek) began with a much narrower ambition. Forth & Towne began as a good idea, but they may have simply run out of money and time to get it right. Starting the next revolution isn't easy.

The Boomlet (Gen Y) Moves into Young Adulthood and Household Formation

Aged 12 to 29, this high-tech generation represents 78 million "connected" consumers. As this group moves through young adulthood and family formation, they will create a surge in the demand for goods and services. Their generational values may be different, the high-tech and mobile way they shop is different, and the products and services available to them will certainly be different, but the family formation life stage is an extremely powerful force at shaping consumer behavior.

Who's reaching this customer today? They are buying their media and electronics from places like Best Buy, but they are also spending plenty of money at Wal-Mart and Target because their dollar goes farther. Stores like Urban Outfitters capture a bit of the counter-cultural edge and, of course, Abercrombie & Fitch (and its many followers) makes a decent official outfitter.

Gen Yers are extraordinarily comfortable on the Internet, both as a source of social networking (Facebook, My Space, You Tube) and as a serious source of commerce. Their immense comfort with technology will make them the early adopters for new technology and disruptive forms of commerce like digital downloading (watch out, media-driven stores).

As the baby boomers get older, however, so do the boomlets. These customers are entering their 20s, getting jobs, and forming families. The retail question is whether these customers will morph into their parents and adopt their buying habits or patterns or turn to new outlets to meet their needs. While there are very clearly "teen" stores, there is not a clear set of stores serving customers in their 20s. This may well be an issue of life stage versus age. Someone in his or her 20s could be married with children and very much adopting the behavior of this particular life stage and shopping at stores of their older compatriots. In a different but similar manner, someone else in his or her 20s could be without a job, living at home, and behaving in a very similar fashion to their teen counterparts—and shopping the same stores. A few chains have begun to experiment with finding that elusive market niche, but a breakout has yet to occur.

As a few examples, Crate & Barrel developed CB2 in an effort to reach younger consumers. The store features brighter and edgier products at lower prices that are more geared to an apartment than a single-family home. The stores are fantastic, in our humble consulting opinion, but they have yet to aggressively grow the concept. Of course, this is part of their standard procedure of growing slow, but it doesn't feel like it's been the hit they were hoping for. Pottery Barn has launched West Elm, their version of shooting at a target (an urban apartment dweller) younger than their main line. In both cases, the life stage component (what type of housing are you living in) feels like the critical driver.

Success in apparel feels even more elusive. Almost simultaneously a few years back, two new start-ups appeared on the scene that promised to appeal to the 20-something customer. MetroPark is the West Coast version, founded by Orv Madden, who had tremendous prior success creating Hot Topic. MetroPark promises a blend of art/music/fashion aimed at the customer who has graduated from Hot Topic and needs hip but more functional clothing. The environment was fantastic, and the early stores showcased smaller brands (Ben Sherman, for one) at higher price points. While MetroPark has expanded, we've also noticed a significant positioning shift. It now seems geared around much edgier urban-type product, appropriate for clubbing and not the workplace. It may be finding a niche, but different from the one originally expressed.

The second start-up came out of Abercrombie & Fitch, the fabulously successful teen retailer that has kept its top spot in the fickle world of teen fashion for nearly a decade. They successfully created the add-on brand, Hollister, by targeting the same customer demographic, but with a slightly different focus. The common denominator for Abercrombie—sex sells. Provide a stimulating visual environment, populate the store with aspirational salespeople (hot young men and women), and position yourself as the premium purveyor in the market. Oh, and create a bit of controversy as often as possible.

The thinking goes, however, that as Generation Y graduates from Abercrombie & Fitch, they will look for more sophisticated styles and price points. Enter a new format Ruehl. In keeping with the Abercrombie & Fitch formula, Ruehl has an inspirational backstory, from the brownstones of New York City's Greenwich Village. Where MetroPark feels like an open block party, Ruehl is an invitation-only retail experience, complete with bouncer (they're sort of greeters) at the door. The major distinction between Ruehl and Abercrombie has more to do with price point than age. Ruehl features more expensive denim to compete against the 7 for All Mankind and True Religion brands and moves into more expensive leather goods. Perhaps the higher price points mean an older consumer. We also think it means a smaller market—Ruehl has not been expanding very aggressively.

We contrast this to their most recent brand, Gilly Hicks, which is the latest in a line of competitors for the nearly monopolistic Victoria's Secret intimate apparel franchise. With Gilly Hicks, we can see the similar brand building characteristics that have served Abercrombie so well. There's the well-detailed backstory—Gilly Hicks was an Englishwoman who moved to Sydney and begin selling lingerie from her home. The store is an effort to preserve that look and feel—dark, intimate, with separate rooms for displaying items. An innovative feature is that each dressing room contains a "library" of most available merchandise for sale in the store so customers can try items on freely. And yes, there is a heavy dose of sex as well, from the provocative photos on the wall to the no persons under 18 allowed on the web site (wink, wink) due to the nudity in the promotional video. Of course, the biggest element that should lead to success will be found in the product itself. It is geared toward a younger woman and seems to compete against the Pink line of Victoria's Secret. In this regard, we would suspect that Gilly Hicks will play well from the Abercrombie & Fitch target of teens through women in their early 30s. And in doing so, it might be able to span a broader age and life stage in the process.

We also believe that globalization will play a significant role in serving this new niche. European fast fashion brands like Zara, H&M, and TopShop seem to effectively be spanning an older age spectrum. As these brands enter the United States with greater intensity, they can also capture some of this elusive market.

Ethnicity Will Drive Segregation and Integration

The numbers are astounding. The country is becoming increasingly ethnic, with enormous growth of Asian and Hispanic populations, now and into the future. What is not as clear are the right actions to support those numbers. At a minimum, retailers need to be sensitive to particular ethnic needs in their assortments. This could run the gamut from size and color sensitivity to items and assortments tailored by store.

The difficulty in executing this lies in the fact that there isn't a homogenous ethnic population. Hispanic tastes are influenced by country of origin, whether it is Mexico, Puerto

Rico, Cuba, or any number of other Latin or Central American countries. Asian tastes reflect the vast diversity of immigration with different needs for Japanese, Chinese, Korean, Philippine, or Thai consumers. Retailers will need to be highly skilled at understanding what is needed for a tailored assortment as well as what will soon be reflected in mainstream tastes.

And if this isn't complicated enough, the country is a huge melting pot. Ethnicities are mixing together, further defying any easy classifications. And, of course, immigration isn't limited to these countries—we are also seeing an influx of consumers from Eastern European countries as well.

New cultural icons span ethnicities with many celebrities enjoying crossover and mainstream status. Ethnicity is greatly impacting what we eat, what we wear, and the music we listen to. The dilemma facing retailers—do you tailor your existing stores or do you create new formats to appeal specifically to an ethnicity? The answer depends on the positioning of your format, the geography that you occupy, and how innovative you want to be. And, of course, whether it will make money.

In supermarkets, as one example, we have seen multiple approaches to ethnic segmentation. Most choose to handle ethnic variety as part of the standard store, changing products, signage, and sometimes décor. There have been mixed results for stand-alone formats—they tend to be highly segmented against a particular population, but chains such as Sedanos in Florida and Fiesta Mart in Texas have prospered.

One of our favorite supermarket chains and a leader in ethnic targeting is HEB. Operating in deeply ethnic Texas (the state is more than half ethnic), they take a multitailored approach to being the best at marketing to the needs of specific demographics. To begin, the company made the decision to operate south of the border stores and has been successfully running them in Mexico for many years. This expertise has enabled them to very effectively tailor stores, when needed, in Hispanic neighborhoods. They run these stores under the HEB banner, significantly changing merchandise, décor, and product mix as appropriate. Not stopping there, they have also developed a dedicated Hispanic prototype called Mi Tienda, which is a fantastic experiential store and is one of the most dynamic supermarkets, of any kind, that we've seen in quite awhile.

We are also going to see a proliferation of Asian formats. One of our favorite specialists is Beard Papa, the Japanese chain that has been opening stores the past few years in the United States. Beard Papa only sells cream puffs, fresh made and filled once you order them. Sound bizarre? The lines outside the door suggest they are on to something. And other Asian imports are headed this way, from the fabulously eclectic Muji to the upscale Famima (convenience stores with Pockys and Paninis).

We expect department stores and other big box stores to continue to tailor more and more to the trade area around each store. The ethnic mix in that trade area will be one of the driving factors in tailoring process. Macy's recently announced, even with a national brand focus, that tailoring to local markets will be critical to future success.

Beyond Demographics: The Significance of Lifestyle, Attitudes, and Values

Demographics and life stages are major contributors to behavioral changes. Societal factors and generational values also play a key role. How people live their lives, what they believe, and how their priorities shift over time have had a major impact on successful retailing ideas and concepts—and on retailing failures as well.

There are a number of important behavioral shifts that have occurred over the past 20 years that are impacting retailing and the development of new ideas and concepts in retailing. We discussed them earlier as part of the inter-connectivity of trends driving change. While some of these behavioral changes are of such magnitude that they merit their own chapters later in the book, some bear brief mentioning here.

Market Polarization

Consumer preference for premium offerings on one hand and no-frills offerings on the other are squeezing out middle-of-the-road products and services. The "average" middle-class consumer—and purchase—is disappearing. Mass luxury items have become more affordable and shoppers trade up to items when they care about quality/prestige (Starbucks). They also trade down to products and services when saving money is more important (Wal-Mart), which allows them to improve their standard of living and/or to trade up again later.

So much has been written about the trading up phenomenon that we're frankly a little tired of it. The well-documented poster child, Coach, has effectively proven that brands can reach a mass luxury level. Many brands strive for this positioning and are aided by strong economic tailwinds that have enabled more and more customers to reach up. At the same time, there are the counter-phenomena of brands becoming too popular for their own good. In other words, the Yogi Berra syndrome of "that store's so popular, no one goes there anymore."

The true "haves"—that 1 percent who have experienced enormous income gains—are looking for more distinctive product that sets them apart. They are searching for exclusivity. Stores like Barneys COOP, Intermix, and Sephora work off the concept of curated consumption. They make their reputation by carrying the next generation of hot brands, leaving the masstige brands to the more conventional department store outlets. Of course, this requires a keen eye for what's hot and the ability (courage) to move out of lines that still could produce significant volume, but no longer offer significant distinctiveness.

Steve & Barry's—Bringing Celebrity Fashion to the Have-Nots

Steve & Barry's is a wonderful example of how wild a path differentiation can take. Although we always like to think of strategic planning and concept development as disciplined, linear processes, the reality is that more companies just "find" their way to success. Steve & Barry's began as small stores in college towns selling licensed athletic sportswear at incredibly cheap prices. Their combination of a clever master licensing agreement of college names and aggressive overseas sourcing allowed them to be a CheapEst store in apparel. They created significant notoriety for selling everything in the store at amazing set price points (indefinite grand opening sales of prices $10 and under, as an example).

As they evolved, a funny thing happened. Real estate became more available, but in many shapes and sizes. Steve & Barry's began taking stores that were three or four or even 10 times their original store size, even moving into older department store spaces. As a side note, this is definitely not the way we recommend growing a chain! (And they have other operating discipline problems as well.) The extra space required extra merchandise and their sourcing expertise allowed them to move into more conventional lines of merchandise, still at great prices.

In a brilliant move, they were then able to arrange a license with Stephon Marbury, a top NBA player, to create a budget line of shoes and clothes. While Marbury is not a top-tier player, he did have sufficient street credibility to make his line of under $20 apparel and shoes resonate at a time when Nike was continually pushing the price envelope upward In 2007, Steve & Barry's launched Bitten, from Sarah Jessica Parker, in women's fashion and has since added a line from Serena Williams as well. All the while maintaining phenomenally low prices.

Obviously, celebrity-endorsed brands are nothing new. Target in recent years has scored considerable points for bringing famous designers like Isaac Mizrahi, Michael Graves, and Mossimo into their fold. But using brands to target have-nots is new. Most celebrity brands are treated as premium lines, however, Steve & Barry's solidified themselves as a solid contender to chains like Gap's Old Navy by bringing this credibility to the masses.

TIME COMPRESSION

Consumers always feel rushed. Many Americans feel their lives are a race against the clock. And it's more than just the lack of time, it is the challenge of managing their lives (and hence shopping) in the small windows of time they have available. Convenience, simplification, and complete solutions are top priorities, as well as utilizing the ease of e-commerce to balance life's demands on time. Retailers offering convenient locations, convenient hours, fast and accurate fulfillment and checkout, and easy multichannel shopping experiences help customers balance their time-constrained lives (and keep them coming back to the retailer).

Walgreens is a classic example of a pharmacy-based convenience retailer whose strategy is to focus on serving the needs of time-compressed customers. In our first book, Walgreens became the poster child of QuickEst, gearing their business strategy around the concept of time and location efficiency. McDonald's has also built their business around the QuickEst concept. And many players have followed suit, offering convenient elements like drive-through windows, 24-hour stores, and home delivery to serve the convenience-driven consumer. We want it now, and we want it fast.

Where will time-compression opportunities avail themselves in the future? We believe technology could play a major role in this arena. The elimination of checkouts would be a huge boost to retailer productivity and customer time savings, and there are programs underway (self-scanning in aisle) that address this. Ultimately, commerce-enabled mobile phones might accomplish the same task. Vending machines from companies like Zoom Systems and RedBox are designed to intercept customers in high traffic locations (airports, train stations, department stores, malls, supermarkets) and offer high-demand items.

From a format perspective, we are seeing a shift back to smaller stores that have convenience as a core proposition. Best Buy has developed Best Buy Mobile in conjunction with CarPhone Warehouse (our first stop any time we hit the United Kingdom) to create wireless retail stores that have convenience as a core proposition. Supermarket retailers are also getting into the act, experimenting with smaller intercept locations. Wal-Mart has announced the opening in 2008 of a 20,000-square-foot format store (a tenth the size of its Supercenters) called Marketside.

Fresh & Easy—Tesco Rocks the Time-Compression Boat

Extremely high on our list of the world's best-run retailers is U.K.-based Tesco, which is currently the fourth largest retailer in the world. After several years spent studying the

U.S. market, they created their format, Fresh & Easy, which they are in the process of rapidly rolling out across U.S. cities. The first major markets included Phoenix, Las Vegas, and greater Los Angeles.

Fresh & Easy is an approximately 10,000-square-foot box that combines several elements that exist in the United States but not in one format. They have the shopping simplicity and convenience size of an Aldi. They have the unique private label of a Trader Joe's, while still carrying national brands. And they promise a new kind of fresh experience, offering prepared foods and perishables with short shelf life through state-of-the-art manufacturing and distribution capabilities.

Early reviews for the format are mixed. They offer a utilitarian and straightforward shopping experience that can definitely save a customer time. But, the fresh side is a disappointment, and it might take a fair amount of time for U.S. consumers to accept packaged products like produce as fresh. There are also the countless details of retail success that can't be underestimated. Do they have the right real estate? The right product mix? The right pricing strategy? And so on.

As in any disruptive format, it is the risk taking of a Tesco that lays the groundwork for the revolution or the next inflection point. They may, or may not, get the small-format store right in the United States. History says don't bet against them. More critically, what countermaneuvers can we expect to see from U.S. retailers who will hardly be passively watching Tesco's invasion. Wal-Mart has already announced their smaller format that will open during 2008 and will create its own stir. Safeway (which has recently opened The Market) and others are also creating responses.

If the consumer trend holds, we expect food retailers will unlock the equation that Walgreen's solved for drug retailing and McDonald's did for fast food.

CUSTOMERS IN CONTROL

Consumers want to be in control of their lives and shopping experiences, especially baby boomers. They want the freedom to be able to shop and buy when they want, how they want, and where they want. The Internet has become a tremendous tool for consumers to increase their overall control of the shopping and buying process. Consumers can obtain complete knowledge about virtually all products and prices and compare and contrast choices. And the Internet is reshaping "word-of-mouth" communication. Consumer advocacy, customer ratings, and customer experience are perceived as more credible, while corporations and the information they provide have become more questionable, leaving consumers with more control and companies with less.

It would be simple to categorize the entire Internet revolution as an example of customers being in control. Indeed, Amazon allows you to shop when you want and does a fantastic job of customizing preferences. EBay is the ultimate in control, where buyers and sellers can dictate what they're willing to pay (although the auction idea has century-old roots). The concept of customers in control is also taking hold in retail, albeit a little slower as stores struggle to change physical parameters and personal process and behavior. Mass customization is beginning to emerge at companies like Build-A-Bear Workshops or at the make your own flexibility of Lush. Customization is beginning to creep into other areas as well, with Nike ID, which allows you to customize a shoe in the store or online, or at Lego, where you can design your own creation. Opportunities still exist though, particularly on the "people" side.

There are several other significant behavioral trends that deserve their own chapters in the book, from our obvious emphasis on green to the shift to experiential retailing. What is certain is that closely watching demographics and resultant behavioral trends and responding to them, is one of the quickest ways to spark a retail revolution.

CHAPTER NINE

Moving Up the Ladder— Growth of Experiential Retailing— How to Drive Sales and Profits beyond Price

We always caution our clients to "beware of the buzzword." When people use the phrase experiential retailing, what exactly are they talking about? A decade or so ago, retailers and restaurant companies became very excited about the notion of "retailtainment." Stores and restaurants were created for the entertainment value and experience quotient. With retailtainment all the rage, entertainment companies joined in as prime participants. Besides the notable and memorable Disney and Warner Bros. stores that had relatively long runs, there were also entries from Ringling Bros., Sesame Street, Viacom, and others. On the food side, who can forget Planet Hollywood, Rainforest Café, Bubba Gumps, and Hard Rock Cafe? But, can you remember the Fashion Model Café?

Clearly, retail and restaurants have to be about the products and services they sell. That's not to discourage entertainment, but to acknowledge that it is simply a piece of the puzzle. What is true is that retail in developed countries is evolving as customers evolve. Going back to Maslow's basic hierarchy, survival depends on taking care of basic needs like food, water, and shelter. As we evolve, our needs also evolve. In a similar vein, we have developed a retailing pyramid of needs as shown in Figure 9.1.

When retailing focuses on a commodity, it really is all about price. Margins get compressed and winners are those who can effectively manage costs. As retailers move up the pyramid and begin to add value to the transaction, price becomes a less important factor. Lifestyle retailers do a great job of focusing on solutions that reduce the commodity aspect of a relationship. At the top of the pyramid is retail's Holy Grail. The experiential aspect kicks in, and customers become considerably less interested in price.

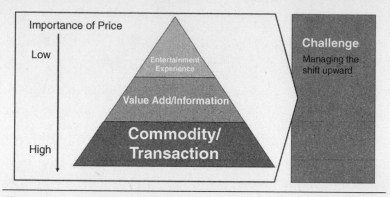

Figure 9.1   Pyramid of Needs

Source: R. Blattberg, Kellogg School of Management. Used with permission.

A great theoretical model, but what does it look like in practice and how can it be replicated across an existing chain or form the foundation for a new one? When we are asked to name lifestyle retailers, the answers come very easily. Retailers from Crate & Barrel in housewares to J. Crew in apparel to Anthropologie in its eclectic glory come to mind. All of these chains do an effective job of targeting specific customers with a clear point of view. They also provide complete solutions to their customers' home or wardrobing needs, not simply items. The list is not simply limited to fashion-oriented retailers—we think Staples is terrific in office solutions and Lowe's in home solutions.

But as we contemplate the retailers who achieve the highest pantheon of "experiential" retail, the list gets shorter. And, admittedly our criteria are probably a little tougher than most. When you think of retailers who transcend retail—they are no longer simply sellers of goods or even solutions—they become a part of people's lives and an integral part of their identity. With that strict criteria, the list does indeed narrow. Yes, Starbucks is a lifestyle retailer that sells more than just a product (coffee), and is also associated with a lifestyle or part of someone's identity. We don't deny (guilty here as charged) that Starbucks may be part of a daily routine or ritual, but we're not sure they occupy the top strata any longer. This may also be why Howard Schultz is back at the helm as CEO—for as good as Starbucks is on so many retail elements, they seem to have lost the intangible experiential piece . . . the neighborhood cafe seems to have inherited the mantle of authenticity.

We define the elements of experiential retailing as follows:

- *Great product:* While this is a no-brainer, it is often an overlooked part of the experiential dimension.
- *Solution-oriented:* Products are organized around the consumers' end use. Rather than having a row of lamps, as an example, solutions oriented retailers like Crate & Barrel or Pottery Barn show the product in vignettes.
- *People as acolytes:* Associates in the store believe they are part of a company with a higher order. They are ambassadors for the brand and are fervent in their jobs. Talk to a Container Store associate and you will see passion that extends well beyond the paycheck.
- *Intense product interaction:* The stores are proud of what they sell and anxious to let the customer find out. The stores are living, breathing demonstration centers, not museums. At the newest T-Mobile concept stores, the

interior is referred to as "the playground"—a place to freely try and get comfortable with new technology.

- *Values-based mission:* It helps if you are a green retailer and are trying to save the world. But having a strong values-based mission works for retailers in a number of areas. Saturn or CarMax salespeople take great pride that their companies are trying to eliminate the bad practices of their industry. Whole Foods is trying to sell better foods—their associates buy into the broader mission.

- *Tight brand group:* Customers feel like they are part of a special group. They are in the know and proud to spread the word. Shoppers at Trader Joe's or Costco know that they are part of something special. But the brand group can't get too large or some of the specialness disappears.

- *Visible identification:* This is not a prerequisite but visibility helps. Whether it's a logo on a bag or shirt or some other visible identification of brand affinity, it's no fun being part of an experiential retailer if you can't show it. When a Harley user tattoos the brand on his chest, it becomes a fairly visible form of brand bonding.

With this set of criteria, few companies score across all dimensions. The obvious candidates are two stores we're a bit tired of writing about—Apple and American Girl. Apple obviously scores on many of these elements but we think a watch-out is on the horizon. We worry for Apple on two dimensions: First, is its brand group getting too large (with a corresponding decline in hipness)? Second, more critically, is it losing its way from a values-based standpoint? In recent months, Apple angered a group of early adopters by radically cutting the price of its iPhone and leaving brand loyalists holding the bag. And just recently, it charged $20 for an iPhone upgrade for software that probably should have been part of the original package. Apple is beginning to sound closer to the folks in Redmond, Washington, than they would like.

How can we pick on American Girl? Easy. While they score high on our criteria in their original stores, we're not as sure about the small store Boutique and Bistro concept they've been opening. Does the experience become less special (and less experiential) in the smaller stores?

So, who else makes the list? There are classic brands that continue to do experiential incredibly well, and Harley-Davidson is one of the best examples. This is about to get even better with the highly anticipated opening of the Harley-Davidson museum—this is a brand that understands experience (though their worry now seems to be about having too much product!). And experiences don't need to be high end to work. Saturn captured that magic over a decade ago, only to get derailed by losing sight of point one—great product.

LULULEMON ATHLETICA—A NEW BREED OF EXPERIENTIAL RETAILER

Lululemon is a Canadian yoga wear retailer that is spreading like wildfire in the United States. We love the store, love the format, and we believe it represents the best of what experiential retailing is all about. They start, of course, with great product. One of their best characteristics is the tag on the product itself, which states, "Why we made this." It then lists the attributes of the product that have benefits to the end user—seamless yoga pants that don't hurt when you lie down on a mat, or yoga instructor pants that make it easier for instructors to demonstrate the right pose, and so on. Of course, all of their customers aren't die-hard yoga fanatics, and the merchandise is organized from comfortable to technical, offering solutions for every occasion.

The retail store is all about touch and feel—all products are out, accessible and ready to try on. The store associates are wearing the merchandise, and they have almost a cult-like enthusiasm for the store's product and the store's mission. There are dozens of bulletin boards showcasing activities. There are customer testimonials abounding. The store's mission is to help customers get out, be active, live life. You don't have to be a hard-core athlete to get enthused by the energy and enthusiasm.

The Lululemon logo and very distinctive (designed to be seen) shopping bag starts the conversation about the brand in health clubs, airports, or in the line at Starbucks. Customers can't wait to share this brand with friends and strangers, and the Lululemon brand is growing without any traditional advertising. It is a great experience.

OOPS—PAIVA DIDN'T DELIVER ON EXPERIENCE

Lululemon is hardly alone in recognizing the trend toward female participation in sports, the growth of yoga, and omnipresent sporting goods stores' male bias. Nike Women, Lucy, Title IX are also competing in this same space. Finish Line, the athletic shoe and active wear retailer, also threw their hat into the ring with the opening (and subsequent closing) of Paiva.

On the surface, Paiva promised many of the attributes of Lululemon. It also attempted to be a lifestyle solution for active women. With Finish Line's background, the store had more emphasis on footwear and on better recognized brands like Nike, Adidas, and Puma. They carried the trendier lines from these manufacturers, but somehow missed on many of the intangibles that separated Lululemon from the pack. In our several visits, we didn't find the store or associates inspiring. Paiva might have served as a functional place to buy shoes and apparel, but missed the higher-order details. Finish Line shut down the concept in 2007.

Who Else Gets Experience?

There are several sporting goods retailers that fulfill the experiential promise. REI perfectly embodies so many of the attributes, from fantastic associates to an environment that fully immerses you in the product. REI's members are part of that self-selecting group who loves the outdoors and they are truly owners of the brand. The stores have great merchandise organized for people who really do climb mountains and kayak rivers—and is not geared just to those who just want to look like they do. Patagonia delivers as well, though without the immersive experience.

In a different vein, Cabela's, the outdoor outfitter, delivers the same magic to hard-core hunters and fishermen. A trip to Cabela's is like a trip to Disney World for their core customers—an immersive environment complete with restaurant and archery range, live stocked fish ponds, and plenty of examples of mounted wildlife. Their customers are a tight-knit brand group, and the store fully understands their needs. Interestingly, Cabela's was primarily a direct marketer before becoming a retailer—the experiential piece added more luster (and considerably more sales) to the brand.

There are other emerging retailers vying for the experiential space. Gilly Hicks may one day qualify, and parent Abercrombie & Fitch's amazing flagship stores absolutely qualify. The passion of customers and associates for the Bare Escentuals brand is nothing short of amazing, particularly since the brand really got its start on QVC. And, their retail stores are among the most productive in the mall. Sephora also captures that magic by being a curator of many hot brands in their stores.

There are also some amazing single stores that create unbelievable experiential environments. Abt Electronics outside of Chicago is almost beyond description. Besides being one of the highest volume stores in the world, it offers a completely immersive and entertaining experience that will have you contemplating major renovations to your kitchen or media room. Jordan Bros. Furniture has several locations, but also has made their reputation on immersive stores.

Spectacular new foodservice brands like Pinkberry, Cupcakes, and Homemade Pizza have developed the cult following of having great products, but we're not sure they deliver (just yet) on the cult experience. Mini could be the new Harley-Davidson or Saturn but they have yet to establish their retail bonafides.

Is there a mass brand that makes the cut? Target (or Tarjay) at times comes suspiciously close. While not having particularly great associates or an immersive experience, spectacular merchandise and great marketing elevate the brand to a special status. Brand stores (to be covered in later chapters) often shoot high to deliver an experience and many times exceed, like M&M World in New York or the Hershey's Experience.

Experiential retailing requires companies to be great on a multitude of dimensions. If companies can reach the summit, however, they have a great chance of revolutionizing their categories.

CHAPTER TEN

GETTING OUTSIDE THE BOX—NEW WAYS TO REACH THE CONSUMER— THE GROWTH OF NONSTORE RETAILING

M ore and more, we hear people talking about brick-and-mortar retailing like it is passé. While it may be true that more people are shopping online than ever (online retail sales in 2007 reached $175 billion, a 21 percent increase over $144.6 billion in 2006, a small part of the over $4 trillion in annual retail sales), traditional physical stores are still the bread and butter of retailing. Yet, it is impossible to deny that there are new and creative ways to engage with the consumer. Brick-and-mortar retail stores aren't going away any time soon, but they will be supplemented by new, outside-the-box (retail store) thinking. In this chapter, we look at new ways to reach the consumer, from intelligent multichannel retailing to pop-up stores.

INTELLIGENT MULTICHANNEL

Almost certainly the biggest revolution in reaching the consumer today is multichannel retailing, or more accurately, *intelligent multichannel retailing.* A multichannel retailer sells directly to the consumer through more than one venue, and an intelligent multichannel retailer successfully integrates the channels so each benefits from the others. The typical historical path taken by a retailer began with a traditional brick-and-mortar storefront or a catalog, followed by a catalog or retail storefront depending on which channel was first, and then establishing a presence online through an e-commerce site as that channel emerged onto the scene. Though typical, this isn't by any means the rule. This is particularly true with the explosive growth of e-commerce, which has proven on many occasions that there is room for "pure-play" online sellers. While there will undoubtedly continue to be pure-play, brick-and-mortar, and direct retailers in the future, the reliance on a single channel significantly misses growth opportunity and doesn't fully enable retailers to maximize the potential of their brand. Retailers should be motivated to establish different channels to reach an entirely different consumer as well as reach existing customers in different, and in some cases, more convenient ways.

Intelligent multichannel retailing involves significant cross-channel influence. In other words, there are a high percentage of customers who have looked for or purchased something previously seen in another channel. The best-in-class intelligent multichannel retailers have made this easy for customers, but to get to this level is challenging, especially when each channel is "siloed," meaning it is operated as a separate business. So why is it so important to achieve cross-channel influence? Because total spending significantly increases as customers shop multiple channels.

JCPenney

The average annual dollars spent by JCPenney customers and the channels they shopped are summarized in Figure 10.1.

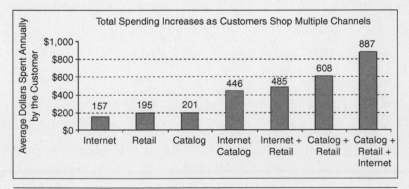

Figure 10.1   JCPenney Multichannel Synergy

Source: JCPenney Annual Report, 2006.

The difference between a customer shopping just the e-commerce JCPenney site and shopping all three channels is a staggering $730 annually per customer. An impressive figure to be sure, even when you consider that their "tri-channel" customers are undoubtedly their most loyal. Not surprisingly, their e-commerce site, JCP.com, is the fastest-growing channel at JCPenney with online sales surpassing $1.3 billion in 2006.

One technique JCPenney uses to convert in-store shoppers to JCP.com is a feature that enables someone online to see whether a desired item is in stock in a selected size or color at a nearby store. As JCPenney plans details for its 250 new stores slated to open between now and 2011, knowing their customer and how they shop will be vital. Last year, Internet-enabled point-of-sale terminals were installed in all stores for even better cross-channel influence.

JCPenney is a best-practice marketer, fully integrating advertising and public relations campaigns in all channels. Based on JCPenney's annual growth in web sales, JCPenney is on track to achieve $2 billion in annual Internet sales by 2010. JCPenney's success is credited to their early, ahead-of-the-game decision to rethink their entire retail model and not treat the Internet opportunity as an isolated business. (It didn't hurt that they already had a well-established direct business through their catalog channel.) They have integrated their web presence throughout JCPenney's stores and catalogs.

JCPenney has also experimented with other new ways to reach the consumer. Coinciding with the company's exclusive retail sponsorship of the Academy Awards, JCPenney constructed a 15,000-square-foot pop-up, or temporary, store at One Times Square in New York City for the month of March 2007. Called the "JCPenney Experience," the store showcased private and exclusive brands. The pop-up store was filled with interactive kiosks that linked customers to their web site where they could search the over 250,000 available items. As with many great ideas, there is a difference between expectation and reality. The pop-up store may have enhanced brand recognition, but consumers didn't engage with the kiosks. Perhaps the most notable thing about this particular pop-up experience is that it was the only place in Times Square that wasn't crowded. The point here is that retailers are still in the nascent stages of figuring out how to really maximize multichannel interactions with the consumer.

Williams-Sonoma, Inc.

Williams-Sonoma, Inc., which operates Williams-Sonoma stores, Pottery Barn stores, and West Elm, has been heralded as an intelligent multichannel retailer. As is the case for JCPenney, Williams-Sonoma's direct channel and specifically the Internet, is the fastest growing channel, with revenues increasing 21 percent to $928 million in 2006. William-Sonoma's mission is to "Own the Home" through multichannel retailing in the highly fragmented home-furnishings market. Their direct-to-consumer (DTC) channel, consisting of catalog and Internet divisions, has served as the platform for the introduction of new brands: West

Elm, PBteen, and Williams-Sonoma Home. The company estimates that 45 percent of companywide (nongift registry) Internet revenues are incremental to the DTC channel, and about 55 percent are driven by customers who recently received a catalog. The catalogs provide advertising material for the stores and the Internet. The mail order catalogs and Internet also are cost-effective ways of testing market acceptance not only for new products, but for new brands.

Williams-Sonoma is constantly working on improvements in the customer channels, but one of the biggest changes they have made is internal. Rather than organize by channel (the norm in most retail organizations), they choose to organize by brand, meaning they make cross-channel decisions for the good of the brand (and potentially at the Profit and Loss expense of a particular channel).

Williams-Sonoma has a full-throttle multichannel strategy integrated into every part of the business. And like JCPenney, Williams-Sonoma's best customers shop all three of their channels.

POPPING UP ALL OVER THE PLACE

New York City's Times Square, Rockefeller Center, Chicago's Michigan Avenue, and other areas with high traffic and visibility are popular places for pop-up stores. We mentioned the JCPenney Experience pop-up store that camped out in New York's Times Square for a month.

A pop-up store is actually not a revolutionary retail idea, but in the past few years it has manifested itself in a chic, almost limited edition way. Today, pop-up stores generate a lot of buzz, bringing brands to life in an exciting, high-rent, temporary environment. Pop-up stores are often used as promotional tools for marketing teams and, because of this, cross over to experiental retail (in these cases, they are more about the brand experience than the selling of goods).

Hickory Farms pioneered multichannel and temporary selling in 1959. The specialty food and gift retailer started by selling their assortment of summer sausage, cheeses, and gift items via catalog, but also setting up temporary booths at fairs and exhibits. They expanded the booth concept by operating seasonal kiosks and temporary outlets in malls across the country. Other pop-up store pioneers include the numerous Halloween and Christmas stores that have built a business on capturing opportunistic space on a seasonal basis.

Considered by many the modern pop-up pioneer, Target caught the attention of the media in 2002 with its 220-foot "Christmas galleries" barge, with bull's-eye-shaped boughs, attached to a pier on the Hudson River in New York City. The next year in September and October 2003, Target opened a 1,500-square-foot store in Rockefeller Center to launch "high-fashion-at-low-prices" designer Isaac Mizrahi's line (and repeated this successful formula for the Proenza Schouler design line, among others). Another seasonal shop, in May–July 2004, Target operated the "Bullseye Inn" in the Hamptons, selling summer goods. Target achieved success on multiple levels—they captured the attention of the key shelter and fashion magazines despite not having a store in Manhattan. They further elevated the concept of cheap chic and sold a few items in the process as well.

The modern pop-up concept has been used as a marketing vehicle for retailers and nonretailers alike. Modern pop-ups can be retailer driven, benefiting from the buzz surrounding it, as is the case with JCPenney and Target. It can also be used as a promotional vehicle, which is the case for supplier and services operated pop-ups.

Suppliers have launched or reinvigorated brands through pop-up stores:

- Looking to "intrigue the young adult urban hipster," Wrigley operated the Altoids Curious and Original Chocolate Shoppes in Chicago's Lincoln Park neighborhood, New York City, and Miami from February 8 through February 14, 2007. Wrigley billed the stores as anti-Valentine's Day shops. According to the company, the stores were for "those exhausted by the unrestrained sentimentality of Valentine's Day. The Altoids Curious and Original Chocolate Shoppe is a haven for the bruised, broken, or blackened heart." Some of the store offerings were, of course, Altoids Dark Chocolate Dipped Mints, but also free coffee and cupcakes, and anti-Valentine's Day cards. With an average of 98 consumers per hour and a total of 20,858 visitors, Wrigley presumably reached its target customer briskly and efficiently.

- Del Monte Foods operated the "Meow Mix Café" in a Fifth Avenue New York 3,500-square-foot space storefront. Meow Mix, a leading cat food brand, leased the space for one month, building out for three weeks, and concluding with the one week run of the café, targeted at cat lovers and their pets. The caféfeatured interactive games for both cats, catlovers, and a gift shop featuring kitty food and cat toys and plenty of sampling of its seven varieties of new Meow Mix Wet Food Pouches. Meow Mix spent a significant amount for such a temporary operation, and it must have been worth it as they have since opened several more cafés.

- Kraft Foods showcased its DiGiorno Ultimate frozen pizza with a pop-up storefront in Chicago's high traffic Michigan Avenue shopping district in summer 2007. The three-day pizzeria served up 25,000 slices a day. The company took it further with a five-city tour in a pizzeria on wheels, juxtaposed with a family kitchen in the back to illustrate the pizzeria quality of the pizza and the convenience of frozen pizza.

Companies other than retailers, like airlines and publications, have used pop-ups to highlight their service offerings. For example:

- In 2003, Delta Airlines debuted their low-cost subsidiary "Song" with a SoHo pop-up that showcased Song's unique offerings including organic food, in-flight TV, radio, and videogames. They operated another Song pop-up in Boston later that summer, sending invitations to target customers, inviting them to try out the new airline through the pop-up store.

- *Wired* magazine took its e-commerce store physical for the 2007 holiday season. The *Wired* store was open from November 16, 2007, through December 30, 2007, in New York City. The store featured a wide range of *Wired*-approved gadgets. It had a multichannel element too with kiosks linking customers to their web site to complete their purchase. The store got a lot of hype due to the special events, parties, guest speakers, and partnership-sponsored giveaways.

Other retailers have gotten into pop-up stores, generally surrounding the launch of a new product or other marketable event, such as:

- Nike opened a pop-up store in SoHo for four days to highlight and debut NBA All-Star LeBron James "Zoom LeBron IV NYC" basketball shoes. 250 special limited edition shoes were priced at $250 each.
- Japanese retailer Uniqlo had a mobile pop-up store for the two months prior to its November 2006 SoHo store opening. Teams drove two shipping containers around New York City, and then popped them open in shopping areas all over the city. According to Shin Shuda, chief marketing officer of Uniqlo United States, "The shipping containers gave New Yorkers a clear message—that we're coming literally from Tokyo to New York."

Retailers acknowledge that pop-ups are clearly a way to generate buzz and reach consumers. How much of it is truly about retail though? Could pop-ups serve as a testing vehicle for e-commerce stores to explore opening a brick-and-mortar store? Bluefly.com, an online retailer specializing in designer clothes at discount prices, has experimented with opening seasonal pop-up outlet stores in New York City. Whether they are doing this to test the brick-and-mortar market is up for debate, but either way they are building brand awareness.

Shopping malls have specialty leasing departments for temporary tenants such as Halloween, Christmas, and calendar stores. Vacant has turned pop-up stores temporary nature into a long-term model. Vacant's retail concept and exhibition store provides space for a month for brands and designers in major cities to sell limited edition and exclusive products—a good idea as pop-ups become more and more popular.

LAUNCHING BRANDS DIRECTLY

Pop-up stores aren't the only ways suppliers are directly reaching their customers. Some suppliers launch their brand without the middleperson. This is also not a revolutionary idea, with brands like Tupperware and Avon using home parties as a way to reach consumers. What's new is the successful introduction of brands through late twentieth-century channels like home shopping networks, infomercials, and, of course, the Internet.

Developed by dermatologists in the 1990s, Proactiv Solution is a three-step acne treatment system that was first sold through infomercials. Celebrity spokespersons helped launch this brand (including Jessica Simpson, Sean Combs, and Vanessa Williams). With brand awareness rising, Proactiv began selling through mall kiosks, smartly reaching their target teenager customer. The multichannel model has been a success, with more than five million active customers and annual worldwide sales of about $850 million.

QVC, the cable home shopping network, launched a national product search that has been called the *American Idol* of retailing. Like *American Idol* winners, there is a tremendous upside potential from being featured as a brand on QVC. QVC considers hundreds of thousands of products annually, winding up with about 180 different products featured daily with new products constantly added to the mix. On August 8, 2001, QVC @ the Mall opened as a flagship store at the Mall of America in Minnesota. As expected, the store featured successful products featured on the networks, and included a studio for live tapings.

Bare Escentuals

Bare Escentuals, the premium cosmetic company, first started in 1976 with a single store in Los Gatos, California, but gained presence through its infomercials and features on home shopping networks. The company's multichannel distribution model consists of infomercials, home shopping television, specialty beauty retailers, company-owned boutiques, salon spas, and online shopping. The company sells its skin-care product lines and focuses on teaching consumers about the benefits of the products through educational media channels.

Operating in the growing beauty market, driven in large part by aging baby boomers, Bare Escentuals' healthier, greener makeup, especially its mineral makeup lines, is trend-right. Accounting for 14.2 percent of net sales, the 51 company-owned boutiques average annual net sales in 2006 was approximately $2,000 per square foot. The company plans to open 35 new boutiques in 2008. The company also sells through specialty retail and department stores, including Sephora, Ulta, Nordstrom, and Macy's.

The majority of Bare Escentuals' sales, however, are derived from infomercials and home shopping television, totaling 45.3 percent. Their informercials, the source for 32.7 percent of annual sales, are broadcast in both 28-minute form programs and 1- to 2-minute short form programs and are designed to sell product through education and also build brand awareness. Launched in 2002, the long-form programs appear on cable networks like Lifetime, Oxygen, Bravo, FX, The Food Network, Style, and Women's Entertainment (WE). During 2006, Bare Escentuals infomercials were broadcast on television an average of over 540 times per week.

Starting in 1997, Bare Escentuals products have been sold through QVC, the home shopping network, accounting for 12.6 percent of sales in 2006. Bare Escentuals began selling a limited product assortment through their e-commerce site in February 2007. The appearances on QVC enhance brand awareness and also help to drive sales to other channels.

Although only 12.6 percent of sales come directly through QVC, the consumer may go to a Bare Escentuals boutique, a retail store, or the Web to make a purchase. Consistent product messaging across all channels leads to the successful multichannel strategy. The physical stores showcase the brand experience and supplement the heart of the business—QVC and infomercials.

The Pampered Chef

The Pampered Chef is another company that has perfected the direct selling route. A direct seller of essential "professional quality" kitchen tools, The Pampered Chef was acquired in 2002 by Berkshire Hathaway, Warren Buffett's well-respected holding company. The Pampered Chef's primary channel of distribution is in-home cooking demonstrations known as "Cooking Shows", with over one million held in the United States each year. More than 70,000 Pampered Chef Consultants, as they are known, perform the in-home cooking demonstrations worldwide. Many have a similar background to the founder—former stay-at-home mom Doris Christopher—who was passionate about cooking and empowered by the flexibility of the entrepreneurial-style job. Founded in 1980 in the basement of her suburban Chicago home, Christopher relied on her experience as a home economics teacher and mother to formulate a plan to sell professional quality kitchen gear directly to consumers through in-home demonstrations. This gave customers the opportunity to experience the products firsthand.

The Pampered Chef has eight levels of field management progressing from consultant to National Executive Director. Of the over 200 products carried, 80 percent are exclusive. The Pampered Chef Test Kitchen develops 400 new recipes and introduces dozens of new products annually.

At the time of the Berkshire Hathaway acquisition, The Pampered Chef had grown into a $700 million enterprise. What presumably attracted Warren Buffett to The Pampered Chef, and what sets it apart from other direct selling models, is Christopher's management style and ability to recruit and motivate the tens of thousands of consultants through handsome incentives (like trips to Hawaii).

Creative Memories

Creative Memories, manufacturer of scrapbooking albums and accessories, is, according to the company, a "relationship business" and a "world leader in memory preservation." Like The Pampered Chef, Creative Memories sells its products directly to consumers through its network of 90,000-plus independent consultants.

The company was founded in 1987 by businesswoman Cheryl Lightle and homemaker Rhonda Anderson as a direct-to-consumer selling structure through "Get Togethers." The consultants work with Get Together hosts and assist with scrapbooking techniques and sell the company's line of products. Driven by a passion for preserving the past, consultants aim to inspire clients through Creative Memories' products by enabling them to archive their families' pastimes.

Creative Memories is an employee-owned company and has consultants in over 10 countries. As is the case with The Pampered Chef, consultants are compensated through sales commissions, and Get Together hosts receive free product in exchange for hosting. These hosts are the principal channel for reaching reach new customers.

Both The Pampered Chef and Creative Memories have continued to innovate as the retail landscape has changed. The Pampered Chef has embraced the e-commerce channel. In 2004, the company launched personal e-commerce web sites for consultants. The company also entered the lucrative wedding registry business via the launch of The Pampered Chef Wedding Registry web site. Consultants have added leverage to the site by becoming regular vendors at bridal expos.

Creative Memories has an e-commerce site that is devoted to digital scrapbooking, a growing trend as more consumers adopt digital photo technology and store photos electronically. All of the Creative Memories products are sold on the e-commerce site; however, the site notes that the "support, encouragement, and advice" customers get from consultants is the key to getting customers' photos and digital prints organized and their stories told. So it is about the relationship as much as the products that makes this direct selling model click.

In a strange sort of synergy, we have lately heard about eco-mom parties started by the Eco-Mom Alliance, where the Tupperware party and book club concept has been replaced by discussions on sustainability and green. They haven't developed a commerce option yet, but we suspect it may not be far behind.

OTHER NON-STORE RETAILING CHANNELS

Vending machines have been kicked up a notch with the rise of vending machine retailing. Vending machines that sell a wide variety of items other than just dispensing food and beverages have been popular in Europe and Asia for years and can now be found in the United States. With the swipe of a credit card, consumers can purchase high-ticket items like Apple iPods from a vending machine in airports across the country and even in Macy's department stores. The technology from Zoom systems has the capability of dispensing products from iPods to high-end cosmetics (including Proactiv Solution). The high visibility of the machines promises both brand visibility and commerce potential.

Redbox will have more installed video rental machines than Blockbuster will have retail locations by year-end, utilizing a simple promise ($1 a day DVDs), an easy-to-use system, and high-profile retail partners from supermarkets to Wal-Mart. Others are working on the promise of 24-hour convenience vending machines (intriguing but yet to be perfected) as well as a host of foodservice options (like pizza or french fries baked to order). In the train station in Amsterdam, as an example, there are fully automated convenience options, and there are attempts in New York City to revive the old automat format.

The verdict is still out on the range of products vending machines can sell. With enhanced technology (such as pay by mobile phone in Korea) and more sophisticated vending options, a world of convenience options could open up for customers in the future. The use of vending to extend store hours or to bring a brand closer to consumers will lead to future innovation.

REACHING CONSUMERS IN NEW AND REINVENTED WAYS

Beyond retail's foundation of brick-and-mortar stores, there are various new and reinvented ways to reach the consumer, and influence and shape the retail landscape. While brick-and-mortar stores' importance will not diminish, the way that consumers can be reached needs to be rethought as their needs change and conventional means to growth become more limited. The reliance on a single format will prove too limiting in the future. Whether it is intelligent multichannel retailing, pop-up, or direct-to-the-consumer retailing, retailers and suppliers need to be open to shaking up their business models.

We are excited about the premise of mobile retailing, about retailing to consumers in their homes and offices, and about intercepting consumers wherever they might be. The growth of retail at hospitals, airports, and a variety of entertainment venues suggests there are many untapped opportunities for innovative retailers and marketers to reach the consumer in a variety of channels in a variety of ways.

CHAPTER ELEVEN

SELLING SERVICES, NOT JUST PRODUCTS

Retailers and manufacturers are conditioned to think of the world from a product-centric point of view. Manufacturers make things, retailers sell things, and customers use them. But customers really don't want things, they want solutions to the problems they have. Some of these problems are fairly straightforward—I'm hungry so I need food, I have a party to go to on Saturday night so I need a dress, and so on. Others are more esoteric—I'm growing older but want to look younger; I'm not feeling well, what should I do; my kitchen is out of date and needs a facelift. In the realm of more abstract problems, solutions can extend in many directions. A customer can buy raw ingredients and make dinner, head to a drive-through fast-food restaurant and have dinner made for them, or perhaps go to a meal preparation center and have premade meals that can be reheated later at home. If interested in healthier meals, consumers may contract with a meal delivery service to have food sent to their house. If they opted for the latter solutions, they have entered into the growing realm of services retailing, where value-added ideas potentially mean greater margins and customer loyalty.

As a way to provide a much broader spectrum of offerings and leverage understanding of their customer, retailers are going beyond products by selling a wide range of services.

Service-based retailing promises to grow in significance for retailers of just about every size and description. These service-based ideas may be components of existing retail stores or stand-alone ideas that might reinvent what a retailer or retail shopping center looks like in the future. Many of these services may not rely on brick-and-mortar space at all. As we move from a Do-It-Yourself (DIY) to a Do-It-for-Me (DIFM) world, we expect to see an influx of retail innovation around solutions and services. Retailers are shifting from *selling products* to *servicing lifestyles*.

DEMOCRATIZATION OF SERVICE

The rich are just like you and me except that they have a lot more money to spend having things done for them. Luxury retailers have long recognized the benefits of value-added services. Barneys, Nordstrom, and Saks have concierge services in some of their high-profile stores. Much like a hotel concierge, in-store concierges provide services such as securing restaurant reservations, arranging car services, and helping get tickets to events. Service staff are also more than willing to offer suggestions for personal shopping, bring clothes right to your home or office, and generally think of creative ways to foster loyalty with customers and generate additional revenues.

We're pretty sure that many customers would appreciate that kind of personal attention, but few have the budget for it. If retailers can figure out a way to mass-deliver service, they can open up a huge and untapped market.

In a home décor magazine, we ran across a Home Depot advertisement promoting their wide offering of home improvement type services, with the tag line, "one finger you don't have to lift." Was this the result of consumers attempting to do their own projects only to learn they took on too much and perhaps it wasn't worth the frustration? We suspect that many factors are at play here, including the fact that services have significantly outpaced retail growth over the past 10 to 15 years. Again, the "haves" have had access to interior design services for quite some time, but Home Depot is attempting to bring these services to the masses.

Demographic shifts have had a big impact as well. Aging baby boomers want to spend more time enjoying life rather than fixing things or finding ways to enjoy it. Consumers in general are more time crunched than ever, which has given rise to a market for more and more services. The decline of the traditional family (think Ozzie & Harriet) and the rise of single-parent households results in a growing need for handyman-like work done by somebody else. Angie's List is a localized member web site devoted to reviewing service companies through unbiased user reports. The lists of services are abundant, and savvy retailers and service businesses seized the opportunity to leverage their brand and capture consumer's dollars by actively pursuing recognition on Angie's List (hopefully scoring high ratings as well). Retail services aren't limited to the home improvement category, however. While some service concepts leave people scratching their heads (A Best Buy day spa?), others have been extremely successful. In this chapter, we examine the main drivers of this trend and who has parlayed offering services right.

"Do It Yourself" (DIY) was a driving force in retailing for many years, and was all the rage in the early part of this century, as television shows like *Trading Spaces* documented the trend, while retailers embraced it. Still, many people's needs weren't met, and "Do It for Me" (DIFM) became the new center of attention for retailers as they sought to innovate and differentiate. We would be remiss not to acknowledge that DIY is largely tied to the real estate market, which has softened. But DIY auto repair and maintenance has also declined considerably over the past 10 years. Autos have become too complex for the amateur to fix, and most consumers don't have the time, nor inclination to save money.

DEMOGRAPHIC SHIFTS

Baby boomers are a powerful group of consumers, with the potential to outspend every other group. It is no wonder retailers are continuously trying to better understand baby boomer needs and meet them. Clearly, boomers are willing to trade money for time. As they have become more financially secure, their needs and spending patterns have shifted away from products and toward services. Price is not the most important factor to boomers in most buying situations, and to many, they would rather just get it done and out of the way than spend a lot of time trying to decide which item or product is just right for the moment. This is particularly true given the fact they are slowly realizing that those moments are numbered.

SERVICES ARE CLEARLY OUTPACING RETAIL GROWTH

A look at industry growth by segment, shows the services industry is growing at a rate of about 7 percent annually, versus merchandise growing at a rate of 5 percent. Much of the service growth has come from increases in health, education, and transportation related services, but home and auto related services as well as beauty services have clearly outstripped the growth in their product counterparts as well.

The DIFM industry is booming. For example, in 2006 Lowe's home improvement stores had over $2.8 billion in installed sales. With a dedicated installed sales team, Lowe's is addressing the needs of customers who prefer to outsource their home improvement projects. Their current in-home selling model positions Lowe's to benefit from the growing DIFM segment, and they are continuing to evaluate other opportunities to increase installed sales.

The Home Depot Home Services business, as well as its Expo Design Centers and Home Depot Design Center test stores, target DIFM customers who select and purchase products and installation services for those products. These installation programs include products such as carpeting, flooring, cabinets, countertops, and water heaters. Despite a tough home improvement market, Home Depot's 2006 retail services revenue increased 8.3 percent to $3.8 billion, a testament to the strength of the services business. We expect home-related services revenue to grow as baby boomers continue to rely more heavily on installation services.

Consumer electronic retailers Best Buy and Circuit City operate home theater installation and consumer PC-related services, Geek Squad and Firedog, respectively. Geek Squad "Total Services" precincts exist in all Best Buy stores. The Geek Squad "agents" wear white short-sleeve dress shirts and black clip-on ties, and drive Volkswagen New Beetles, dubbed "Geekmobiles." Best Buy services make up 6 percent of total revenue, but it is clearly a growing piece of the business. Likewise, Circuit City's Firedog service offers consumer solutions with the slogan "Have no fear, firedog is here." While still a small part of total revenue (hovering around 1 percent), Circuit City estimates a $20 billion consumer market opportunity for these services by fiscal 2010. More importantly, these types of services are considerably less price sensitive than retail products and have much higher margins as well. While consumer electronics retailers are busy beating their brains out on who can sell computers or plasma TVs at the lowest prices, they are also waking up to the fact that customers are really unhappy if they can't make that fancy home theater work or get their wireless network turned on and working as promised. Service-based retailing isn't just a nice to have;

it might represent the reason why certain chains stay in business. Circuit City and Tweeter are retailers hovering on the brink—their survival may depend on transitioning their business to services and solution-based selling.

With over 80 percent of their customers classified as business customers, office suppliers like Office Depot and Staples have smartly added office services to their mix of solutions. Staples Copy and Print Centers offer services for both businesses and regular consumers, such as photocopying, binding, labeling, and shipping services with UPS. Staples' in-store Copy and Print Centers accounted for 5.1 percent of North American retail revenue in 2006. They are also testing stand-alone copy and print stores to compete with copy center market leader FedEx Kinko's, which currently holds about 10 percent of an estimated $20 billion market. Recognizing the profit potential, Office Depot is renovating its retail stores to make copy centers more visible to customers near the front of the store.

PetSmart and the "Humanization" of Pets

PetSmart has experienced significant growth as a result of the introduction of selling services like day care and overnight care, grooming, training, and full-service veterinary hospitals within stores. In 2005, the company changed its name from "PetsMart" to "PetSmart" and with this change, its mission, too. PetsMart was a place where consumers could get everything they needed for any pet. PetSmart is a place where pet parents feel they can go to ensure that they and their pet have the best available care. According to the company, "TLC" means Total Lifetime Care for pets and parents.

They are no longer saying to their customer: "We have every kind of pet food and supply you can imagine." They are now saying "What issues does your pet have, and how can we help to make sure you and your pet are well taken care of?" As facilitators of care, they recognize that people's relationships with their pets have changed and they have adapted their stores to facilitate this change.

PetSmart created PetsHotel as a full-service in-store boarding facility for dogs and cats in 2005, opening their 100th location in February 2008, with plans to ultimately roll out 435 PetsHotels. The PetSmart services business is growing at a rate of over 20 percent annually, with more than 10 percent of their total sales in 2007 coming from the selling of services.

Extending the PetSmart brand to services has worked, and the rise in pet ownership and the humanization of pets has proven profitable. The PetsHotel mission is "focused on providing superior care and personalized attention for all pet guests so pet parents have peace of mind that their pet is safe and happy." In some PetsHotels, "Pawsidential services" are being tested. Premium Pawsidential services include bedtime stories and belly rubs. And for those pet parents who want to check in on their pet, they can call in and hear their pet bark or meow through a speakerphone.

Softer Side of Services

Grocer Publix introduced its Apron's program offering services such as in-store cooking demonstrations, a cooking school with food preparation classes, easy-to-use weekly recipe cards with photo lists, shopping lists organized by store department, and even the utensils and cookware needed for meal prep and serving. Apron's Make-Ahead Meals program lets customers assemble meals in the in-store Apron's kitchen with premeasured ingredients and customizable portioning. Apron's facilities are large enough to accommodate groups, turning the Make-Ahead Meals program into a wholesome experience aimed at bringing families back to the kitchen table. Publix clearly knows their busy and older customer and obviously is addressing their unique needs. As the company's web site explains, "In today's hurried world, it can feel next to impossible to prepare a meal at home. But thanks to the experts at Publix Apron's, you can still enjoy the fun of cooking and the togetherness of a family dinner."

Food service and restaurants have been growing within supermarkets for the past 15 to 20 years. Recognizing the fact that consumers don't know how to cook from scratch, much less have time to do so, food retailers have expanded their food service operations to capture a larger share of the consumer's stomach. In fact, a recently opened Whole Foods in the Phoenix area has been dubbed a "groceraunt," a combination grocery store and restaurant, because it offers such a large variety of mini-restaurants and food service operations. Food services, if done right, differentiate a retailer from competition and add precious margin dollars to the bottom line.

Beauty care offers services opportunities as well. In April 2006, Coldwater Creek seized the opportunity to break into the highly fragmented spa business. Coldwater Creek targets women between 35 and 60 with an average income of $75,000 with its line of clothing and accessories. The company describes its customer profile as "a professional woman, 35 to 60 years of age. She is educated, has more discretionary income than free time, and uses our retail stores as a place to get away from it all—while she shops. She also enjoys the ease and convenience of e-commerce and catalog shopping." Now with eight spa test locations, it sounds like she enjoys getting away from it all, while she shops and buys services, too.

Whole Foods Market recently opened a spa in Dallas, Texas, not too far from its company headquarters in Austin, Texas. The full-service Refresh spa, housed in a 4,500-square-foot space above the main floor of the market, is about servicing the "well-being" of its customers. The spa features an on-site nutritionist, naturopathic doctor, estheticians, and massage therapists, and services including massage, waxing, facials, makeup consultation and application, and personal nutrition and wellness consultations. At the same location, concierge services abound. Menu planning is available for $20 per hour, dietician consulting for $100 per hour, and personal shopping for $20 per hour, to name a few. Whole Foods Markets emphasize high-quality products and positions itself as a lifestyle brand. They also opened a San Francisco location with a mini-spa, with many of the same features as the larger, original spa. All products used in both spas are selected based on a stringent set of quality standards. This might not mean much to some spas, but consumers are familiar with and have come to trust Whole Foods quality standards, which means a big head start for the spa.

While spas are nothing new, spas that can effectively offer services to the masses can greatly expand the market.

Retail Clinics—Affordable Diagnosis and Cure in One Spot

Providing proper and cost effective health care may just be the biggest political and social issue in the United States today. Retail stores have played a critical role in this business but historically on the product end—prescription and over-the-counter drugs have experienced exponential growth, and retailers are great sources for the stuff needed to take care of medical issues. But, as retailers look at the broader issue of wellness, their role is likely to expand greatly in the future. The almost meteoric growth of retail clinics is just one of these areas.

By definition, a retail clinic is a health service operation that offers limited-scope, general medical services to the public on an ongoing basis within the space of a larger retailer. Largely staffed by nurse practitioners in collaboration with an off-site physician, most patient visits last 15 to 20 minutes with no appointment required, and price ranges usually between $40 and $70. Many of the clinics also accept insurance.

The market forces behind these clinics, which are estimated to total between 1,500 and 1,800 by year-end 2008, include ineffective primary care delivery, health-care cost pressures, and the forever growing need for convenience. Consumers' use of retail clinics serve as a substitute for routine doctor visits and include vaccinations, common medical diagnosis, wellness screenings, and physicals. As a result of visits to retail clinics, 80 percent to 90 percent of the retail clinic patients fill their prescription at the retailer's pharmacy, with an average prescription price of $30.

According to the Convenient Care Association, about 7 percent of Americans have tried a medical clinic at least once.[1] This evolving industry has a way to go before all the dust settles around policies, but retailers are forging ahead with moderate success.

Wal-Mart is one of the big players in the health-care space with 78 clinics as of February 2008 and plans to have 400 in-store clinics by 2010. Target has retail clinics in 18 of its Minnesota stores and five of its Maryland stores. Drugstore rivals CVS and Walgreens opened over 700 clinics between December 2006 and February 2008. This rapid expansion has not been without problems or uneven performance. Retailers generally operate retail clinics in partnership with various local health-care providers. In July 2006, after 18 months of working with MinuteClinic as an outside operator, CVS acquired MinuteClinic. According to the company, the decision to acquire MinuteClinic was driven by their belief that it was the best concept for consumers, payers, and providers (and that they wanted control of the operations to ensure more consistent delivery).

The value proposition for retailers is two-fold. First, retail clinics drive revenues by increasing customer visits and the time they spend in the store, drive pharmacy and over-the-counter businesses, and enhance loyalty with new, value-added service. Second, retail clinics decrease store operating costs through lower health-care costs for employees and through decreased absenteeism. And, in a somewhat ironic combination of a problem meeting an opportunity, retail employees are among the least insured and most time-pressed consumers. They may well be the best customers for their own clinics.

Financial Services

Umpqua, a banking chain in the Northwest, makes a conscious effort to blend financial services with retail. Their locations are not called branches, but "stores", with a flagship branch in Portland, Oregon that looks more like a hotel lobby than a financial institution.

One of the innovative ways that Umpqua has integrated retailing with banking is through design. Their flagship store was engineered by Nike headquarters' architects Thompson Vaivoda & Associates with an interior by Ziba Design. The result is a space that encourages customers to linger at the bank rather than use ATMs. The redesign also encouraged customers to leave larger competitors, and as the bank's deposits increased, bank executives from around the country began to take notice. This redesign also earned Umpqua the Industrial Design Excellence Award.

The newly designed bank branches have the look and feel of retail stores complete with branded merchandise. Umpqua pioneered the bank-cum-cafe trend in featuring computer cafes that allow customers to sip Umpqua Bank-brand coffee while reading the paper or paying their bills online.

Umpqua Bank's Private Client Services Division provides tailored financial services and products to individual customers. The checking programs or "banking blends" are designed to cater to target groups. For example, "go" for those who are 18 to 25, "cruise" for over 55, and so on. Umpqua goes beyond typical banking services by incorporating social services like throwing free Friday night movies, yoga classes, and home-improvement workshops. The bank also provides after-hour use of the space for community activities such as investing club meetings, poetry readings, and seminars on how to buy art.

Umpqua Bank is in continued talks with Microsoft to incorporate technology concepts with the potential to change the way people bank. Innovative approaches to customer service include enabling a customer's personal digital assistant (PDA) or cell phone to send an identifying signal to bank associates when they enter the store. The associate can then quickly begin the process of accessing the customer's account to help reduce wait times.

The Discover Local Music program is another example of how Umpqua Bank is redefining the way it interacts with its customers. The program includes a *music identity*, which connects Portland customers with the sounds of the city's music scene by using a visual in-store display. As part of a welcome kit, new customers can pick songs from the variety of music available on Umpqua's Discover Local Music Catalog and create a free custom CD. Umpqua worked with Rumblefish, Inc., a Portland-based music identity and licensing company, to develop the Discover Local Music program.

SO WHAT'S NEXT?

Retailing has just scratched the surface of the opportunities for expansion into service-related businesses. Peruse any big strip center or shopping center and you might see the following:

- Weight loss or weight control centers from Jenny Craig or Weight Watchers. We expect to see retail stores create or incorporate wellness and diet programs into their stores.

- Meal preparation centers like Dream Dinners and Dinners by Design are driving ideas like Publix's Aprons.

- Kroger and Loblaws have experimented with fitness centers in their supermarkets, and concepts like Curves occupy numerous locations.

- Blue Cross Blue Shield of Florida has opened health insurance "stores" in Florida to educate and sell consumers on their services.

- Financial planning centers are opening to help baby boomers plan for retirement. Some will be from expected providers like Charles Schwab—others will be from banks and other institutions, such as insurance companies.

- Brite Smile has teeth whitening "stores" in many markets. Expect to see huge growth in convenience-based beauty services from the routine (nail salons) to the more complex (laser hair removal).

- David Weekley Homes has opened up showrooms in many of their markets to help new home buyers select the appliances, carpeting countertops, lighting, and other finishes that go into their new homes.

- The next big thinking right now is wellness, and sleep problems are getting a lot of attention. Sleep management retail services would provide sleep consulting and sell sleep products and solutions.

We think there is no end to viable service extensions to existing businesses or the entrepreneurial development of new ones. All retailers need to take a long look at their current business model to determine if there is further value that can be offered to customers. What are customers doing themselves that you could be doing for them? And where do retail services play in your future?

CHAPTER TWELVE

BRANDS GOING RETAIL—THE BATTLE FOR CONTROL OF THE CUSTOMER

Great brands will survive. Some will be owned by retailers, some by manufacturers, and some jointly controlled by both.[1]

—*Ted Zittell*

There were simpler times in retailing. Brands manufactured products and distributed them to retail stores. Brands were good at making things, promoting things, and bringing customers to retail outlets to buy them. Retailers, in turn, were good at distributing items through their system, displaying products, and operating stores efficiently. Two different worlds and two very different skill sets.

Like Icharus flying too close to the sun, neither party was ever particularly content with this arrangement. Retailers often operate on razor-thin margins where brands can earn considerably more. Naturally, if a retailer can replace a brand with its own label, more margins and profits come directly to the bottom line. Brands, in the meantime, covet a retailer's direct relationship with the end consumer and are under a fair amount of pressure to grow and produce higher margins themselves. Their retail clients, however, are getting bigger, exerting more control and squeezing out that excess envied margin. And retailers don't take enough of their product, display it right, or sell it right. If a brand could eliminate the retailer, the brand could create a better impression with the customer. Thus the battle lines are drawn.

Historically, there have been retailers who acted more like brands. Sears was one of the pioneers of sophisticated private branding, and lines like Kenmore and Craftsman have become brands in themselves. And Sears was rewarded handsomely with market share and increased margins. But the magic of those brands certainly didn't translate uniformly into categories like apparel and home. The Great A&P (their adjective, not ours) was a significant manufacturer and seller of their own products (Eight O'Clock Coffee) until national brands made the A&P offer increasingly less competitive. And brands have also dipped their toes into the retail arena. Outlet retailing has been an accepted form of brand extension for many years, and luxury suppliers

(Louis Vuitton, for example) often control their own retail distribution points.

From a mainstream retail standpoint, the push of brands developing direct relationships with consumers is relatively new. While this was once the purview primarily of luxury brands, today we find brands of all types and sizes are relying more on retail channels to reach their core customers. We see this across almost every category, from apparel and accessories to electronics, toys, food, and personal care.

BLAME APPLE (OR COACH), BUT BLAME SOMEONE

The very notable successes of an Apple or Coach with their retail forays have only heightened the (often misplaced) desire for brands to enter into the retail arena. In both these instances, the brands have done something rather miraculous. They have developed a profitable retail chain and have maintained or grown a prosperous supplier business. In fact, their success at retail has led their brands to become more desirable. Desirable brands are a good thing—it allows them to have tighter control at retail, which protects assortments and pricing strategies.

But for every Apple or Coach, there is a Dell, Gateway, Liz Claiborne, or Kate Spade—strong brands that did not translate well into retail. There are a few rules that need to be followed before contemplating a retail entry, along with some practical advice for brands entering the retail arena:

- *Ad campaigns come and go.* Retail stores are permanent (or semi) and have monthly rent and payroll obligations that don't go away. Yes, they can be great for brand building, but are also very costly to consistently implement at a large number of locations.

- *A brand is not a store.* Stores offer consumers solutions while brands typically sell product. Just because you have products doesn't necessarily mean you have all that is needed to solve a customer's problems. Space, personnel, and physical availability are experiental values that stores offer and brands typically do not.

- *The stronger the point of view of the brand, the better the store.* There are many very successful brands that don't make good stores. Instead, they make good components of other people's stores, filling out assortments but not capable of standing on their own.

- *Retail is detail, and it's hard.* Successfully running retail stores requires a myriad of skill sets (systems, operations, customer service, retail marketing, replenishment, etc.) not inherent in a manufacturer. While retailing may look easy, these details trip up many brands (and retailers) themselves.

We are certainly going to see more brands entering the world of retailers and more and more retailers acting like brands. Successful brands (we call them Super Brands) have the operating abilities of a retailer and the product development skills of a brand. They are formidable indeed, and their skill sets can create a revolution in retailing. These companies will gobble up market share and have competitive advantages that a single point of view purveyor won't be able to provide.

In traditional marketing speak, skill sets were always referenced as the 4Ps—product, place, promotion, and people. While the Ps have changed a bit over the years (you will often see price listed as a discreet P), the basic premise held—suppliers worried principally about product and promotion and retailers fretted about people and place. This model doesn't hold up in a more complex world, and Super Brands have a bewildering variety of Ps at their disposal. Today's Ps also include new concepts like:

- *Patterning and projection*: Patterning refers to the ability to spot macro-trends and create businesses out of them. Abercrombie & Fitch was adept at studying the beach culture of California and developing the lifestyle brand Hollister. Fashion brands and athletic footwear brands study trends among inner city youth to gauge where the next fashion or sneaker trend will emerge. Projection refers to the ability to take a niche trend that exists among a select group of consumers and create a mainstream opportunity. Time and again, consumer electronics brands demonstrate ways to grow market size by finding new uses and new demands. It was Thomas J. Watson, then IBM chairman, who in 1943 predicted that there was a world market for about five computers. And soon, we believe, marketers will be the ones to determine the right way to position electric vehicles for more mainstream use.

- *Positioning*: As we have discussed in prior chapters, positioning means expressing a point of view and standing for something specific against a set of targeted customers. The notion of -EST rests on positioning—owning something in the customer's mind. While this concept is second nature for brands, it often strikes retailers as a bit odd. The counterpoint to selecting some customers means that you want to fire others. Many retailers are loath to give up on any customer group—those are usually the retailers who end up in the black hole.

Any complete picture of a sophisticated brand/retailer marketer looks something like the example in Figure 12.1.

The challenges of becoming a superior modern-day marketer aside, we expect an explosion of manufacturers entering the retail business. The pace of change in retail remains rapid, presenting both opportunities and challenges. Existing patterns of distribution, presentation at point of sale, sell-in, and sell-through aren't working well enough for many brands. Many brands are reaching an inflection point, requiring major shifts in distribution strategy. For some, it means testing branded retail, while for others retail can

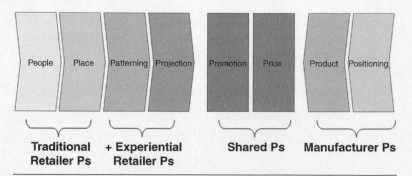

Figure 12.1   Sophisticated Brand/Retailer Marketer

become not only the primary growth driver, but also the biggest revenue contributor. There is value to be added at retail, and brands feel they have a right to receive the profit rewards that go with that added value. Make no mistake, the stronger the brand and the stronger the retail format, the more profit there is available. Simply put, brands are always going to be attracted to gaining a bigger share of the pie. Vertically integrated retail or brand organizations make more money—and that's not a bad reason to get involved.

WHY DO BRANDS GO RETAIL?

Brands are increasingly looking at options that provide faster growth and greater control of their products. For some brands, retail becomes a critical revenue driver, while for others it is primarily about marketing and brand positioning. Retail can also be an effective channel for measuring consumer response to new products, brand extensions, new concepts, and new experiences.

The need for greater control over managing growth and establishing a direct relationship with target consumers is understandable given the many challenges facing brand manufacturers and distributors today. Several pressure points are driving manufacturers to become retailers, including:

- *Fewer stores*: Consolidation and the decline in the number of store locations can mean fewer distribution outlets. Apparel and accessories brands have been hit hard, both by consolidation within the department store segment, but also by the rapid expansion of vertically organized specialty retailers. Consolidations are also affecting brands in many other retail segments, such as sporting goods, supermarkets, and drugstores.

- *Survival of the fittest*: Dominance of one or two key retailers at the expense of competitors can also leave little room for growth through multibrand retailers. Best Buy in consumer electronics and Bed Bath & Beyond in home fashions are widening their lead over the pack. The list of struggling competitors is long, from Radio Shack and CompUSA to Pier 1 and Linens 'n Things. Coupled with retailers' growing demands for exclusives, this often leaves brands battling with competing objectives instead of focusing on innovation and growth.

- *Growing niches*: Brands are also increasingly acquiring smaller, niche brands to drive topline growth. Often these niche brands have limited distribution, and branded retail can be an effective way to build brand awareness. Liz Claiborne has a stable of 25 brands, many with their own retail channel. VF Corporation, Jones Apparel Group, Samsonite, Nike, Adidas, and many others have been acquiring smaller brands.

- *Changing conditions*: Many factors can affect established distribution patterns: rapidly shifting competitive and consumer behaviors impact retailers' choice of preferred suppliers. Some retailers demand increasing and often one-sided concessions. New trends and attitudes about in-store presentation and marketing may not effectively communicate a brand's vision to the consumer, and retailers may not provide adequate service or support.

- *Stricter retailer controls*: New technology or financial goals can lead to lower inventory or tighter assortments. Vendor matrices can keep a brand out, while small and newer brands may find it hard to get an audience with a retailer, much less an order. And retail consolidation has left a much more powerful set of retailers who can leverage their size to exercise more control of the distribution process.

- *Exclusivity*: Couple these factors with the trend of department, discount, category killers and supermarket chains toward private labels and exclusive brands, and it is easy to understand the interest in "going retail."

Brands have a number of options in looking at retail space. Key areas include:

- *Flagship stores*: These are typically experience stores in high-profile retail locations designed to boost brand image and awareness (but not necessarily make any money). Nike probably started the flagship trend but it has been duplicated by scores of brands including Hershey's, M&M World, Garmin, and many others.

- *Full-line stores*: These stores are designed to provide a blend of brand building and commerce. Apple would be the poster child of this trend, successfully doing both. Many apparel brands (Polo, Timberland, Cole Hahn) have adopted this strategy as well as cosmetics brands (MAC, Origins, Aveda, Kiehls) and others.

- *Shops within shops and kiosks*: There are many variations on this theme, from being a tenant within an existing store to a shared space arrangement.
- *Outlet stores*: Dozens of brands operate outlet stores, which have proven to be both excellent sales and profit builders. Today's outlet stores, though, often have the look, feel, and finish of a full-line store.
- *Pop-ups*: Pop-up stores are temporary stores designed to create buzz for a limited period of time. Brands like Method, Illy, DiGiorno, and Meow Mix have opened pop-up locations. Other brands like Motorola have dabbled with temporary retail pop-ups that exist for only a few weeks.
- *Experiences*: Brands have also opened experience extensions (Mr. Clean car wash), hotels (Bulgari, McDonald's, Miss Sixty), restaurants (Weber, Harley-Davidson Café), spas, and the like.

Other examples of successful brands going retail include Maytag Appliances, which introduced its Maytag stores in 2003. The stores are designed to showcase Maytag products offering a boutique-like format that allows consumers to "test-drive" appliances before buying. Customers can run a load of their dirtiest laundry or bake a favorite dish.

Illy, an upscale brand of coffee, took an innovative approach to pop-up retailing. Open for just three months in SoHo Galleria, Illy was designed to look like an art gallery with a small espresso cafe. The centerpiece of the store was a coffee cup sculpture/chandelier. Colorful espresso makers were displayed museum style with a live, interactive play developed exclusively for the store.

Nike has extended their brand with NikeWomen, which features a lifestyle-driven approach to women's performance athletics to serve women customers in a more intimate and focused way than in their bigger stores, the catalog, or web site. NikeWomen also is positioned to make money, taking conventional retail locations and dialing down some of the experience of earlier NikeTowns.

The American Girl store is an elaborate retailing experience, entertaining shoppers for hours and garnering frequent return visits—or should we say, major expeditions. With a theater (in the process of being removed), hair salon, nursery, doll hospital, and elegant sit-down restaurant in the store, in addition to the extensive collection of dolls and accessories, American Girl has become a major destination. The store seamlessly blends commerce and experience, creating memories for a lifetime.

WHAT'S NEEDED FOR LONG-TERM SUCCESS?

We believe there are several criteria that any successful branded retail concept should meet:

Put customers first: These stores offer something different that customers can't get elsewhere, whether it's product, information, experiences, or a combination of all of these. Such stores have an energy and vitality—an edge—that sets them apart. Being successful requires clearly identifying and understanding the target customer and delivering exactly what he or she wants.

Have an edge: There must be a reason for the brand to exist as a direct-to-consumer retail concept—it should fill a void or do something better than any other retailer offering that brand. Positioning the brand in an exclusive setting must answer a true need for today's time-starved and ever-more sophisticated consumer.

Brand distinctiveness: We would like to develop a brand-o-meter, a computerized tool that could magically answer the question as to whether a brand has what it takes to succeed. Take the example of Dell and Apple. We all know about Apple's retail success, but what about Dell. Arguably, Dell was just as well known (and considerably bigger) than Apple when they entered retail. But, Dell suffered from both a lack of inspiration and execution. Dell first opened kiosks, but surprise, they couldn't actually sell anything. Dell wanted to maintain (and perhaps rightly so) their model that is built around custom-developed product and a tax-free sales proposition. Even when they did open a "real" retail store, it still disappointed customers. Why? There was nothing distinct about the store or the brand. Close your eyes and visualize what Dell should look like as a retail entity—and therein is the problem. Dell has since expanded their distribution within other people's retail stores—probably the right decision.

Profitability: The concept should be executed profitably as a retail business. Successful retail concepts are a win/win proposition for the customer and the brand. There is something about making money that ensures concepts work better than if they are purely envisioned as an advertising vehicle.

Execution: Perhaps the most significant hurdle is an organization's lack of retail experience, expertise, and culture to lead the move to retail. Brands just don't operate under the same culture as retailing. Dealing directly with consumers is different than dealing with business accounts. To be successful, this almost always means bringing in experienced retail executives and building new capabilities.

Success as a brand does not guarantee success as a retail concept. We believe the brands that are winning as retailers invest heavily in cultural change, positioning, planning, and supporting retail as a means to better serving its core customers. Apple has already created one retail revolution—we are poised to see other brands, in other categories, make the same sort of history.

CHAPTER THIRTEEN

12 Rules of Successful Retail Innovation

A lthough this title is eye-catching (or so we hope), there really is only one rule that matters—make money and survive. Too many new concepts are beautifully designed and highly creative in their execution but almost destined to fail. Why? Somewhere along the way, there is a fatal flaw that dooms what was otherwise a promising idea. Unfortunately, in retail there are a multitude of things that must go right (and the stars must be perfectly aligned) to really make the new idea or concept work successfully.

The 12 rules, almost like a legal document, also have some subrules and lots of caveats along the way. Twenty-plus years of empirical history and experience in helping retailers and suppliers create new concepts have helped develop the list, but the pitfalls are still everywhere. With that appropriate amount of caution, here's what matters as a minimum:

1. *Look for consumer tailwinds*. We have devoted several chapters of this book to relatively detailed discussions on the key demographic and behavioral changes we see happening among consumers. And for good reason—putting the customer first is the foundation for successful retail formats. Tailwinds are also critical—it is easier to launch a new idea that is in tune with future consumer demand than one that fights it. Successful ideas and concepts pay close attention to what is happening with customers and ride the tailwinds. We have spoken about aging consumers, increasing ethnicity, the have and have-nots, and so on. Chances are that any new idea that works will capitalize on one of these big consumer trends or the resulting behavioral changes (wellness, time compression, etc.).

2. *Scan the competitive world very carefully*. It almost goes without saying that retailers and suppliers must pay very close attention to their direct competitors. But it is also surprising how many competitors they miss or fail to recognize early enough. Watch competition closely and with great respect. And expand the definition of competition broadly. Include both close-in competition and indirect competitors—that's where the revolutionary change is more likely to

happen. And, it is now more critical than ever to pay attention to global competition. The U.S. apparel industry should have reacted much more rapidly to fast-fashion trends that swept through Europe. Hypermarkets across the world presaged the growth of supercenters. What trends now are occurring around the world that will shake up North America?

3. *Understand your own competencies.* Whether you're an entrepreneur or a Fortune 50 company, work hard to understand your own strengths and weaknesses. We are surprised, again and again, how this simple adage is often ignored. Some of the largest companies in the world have conveniently ignored that they had no internal skills in a business they were about to enter. And huge suppliers have underestimated the resources necessary to run a retail store. Entrepreneurs also have similar blind spots—they may be extremely strong on product development but have zero financial skills. They mistakenly believe that great merchandise will help overcome a lack of operating disciplines. Know your own strengths and weaknesses. Then, shore up those areas where you know you're going to need help.

4. *Embrace the notion of positioning.* Positioning makes you declare who you want to serve, against what set of competitors, with what unique benefits you will deliver. At McMillan|Doolittle, we call it -Est positioning, determining what you will be best at. The

flip side of -Est is also declaring who you won't serve, who you won't be competing against, and what you will be giving up. While most new concepts have little trouble declaring what they want to be great at, they also seem to have a hard time giving much up. The courage to specialize is a key notion of positioning. Finally, don't forget the "wow" factor. We have seen more consumer focus groups than just about anyone and in more categories as well. A common new concept belief is "the current market need is not being met." The consumer point of view is "things are just fine the way they are." Sure, they could be better, but most customers don't stay up nights worrying about the minutia that retailers are obsessed with. If you want to make change, make it big, make it noticeable, and make it a "wow." In order to do this, stay open to all ideas at the beginning. As part of our concept development process, we engage in ideation exercises that are designed to stretch thinking. It is hard to get out of the box, but that is critical if you want to carve out new space.

5. *Think through the customer experience.* One of the more productive steps we build into our concept development process is to engage in customer experience management exercises. We call it customer experience blueprinting. Simply put, this means developing a number of scenarios that a customer might experience in the store and then walking through the steps of

how their problems will be solved, how they will interact with associates in the store, and how we can turn something problematic into a unique solution. These visualization exercises help predict how that store can better function in the real world. We really love stores that have thought through meeting the needs of their customers—these are concepts that start to climb along the continuum of selling stuff to understanding and selling to a lifestyle. They also have a better shot at getting to that elusive step of becoming an experiential store.

We often talk about building a "back story" about the brand that defines the essence of the brand, why the brand exists. Some brands have naturally strong back stories about their history and founders (Sam Walton at Wal-Mart, Gordon Segal at Crate & Barrel, etc.). These brands have their essence baked in, but that doesn't mean they don't need reinforcement now and then. Other brands can create a fictionalized back story (Hollister or Gilly Hicks) that helps to define what the brand is trying to achieve.

6. *Have a sound business plan.* We are unabashedly pro consumer (revisit rule number 1), but we have also learned through hard experience that fundamental business planning is absolutely critical. Solid financial planning includes understanding and validating each set of assumptions that go into a plan. Take sales projections, as one example. We work through

these numbers from a top-down and bottom-up perspective. It is easy to say that a store should achieve a certain amount of sales per square foot based on what similar competitors do. But, this sort of assumption misses a basic point—sales are built one customer and one transaction at a time. Do the math to understand what it takes to meet the numbers. How many sales per hour, selling what, at what transaction size, during what hours, and so on. Done this way, it brings a healthy dose of reality to assumptions. The same exercise needs to occur for every single number on a profit and loss statement, so they are not just figures on a spreadsheet but the understanding of what makes a business tick.

7. *Create an effective store design.* Effective may seem like a strange word here. And, it may seem a bit unusual that design is relatively far down on the list of key steps. Store designers aim for breathtaking and brilliant. They want dramatic presentations and unique signature elements. While a good design is critical, customers don't buy store design, they buy merchandise and services. Design and services should complement but never overwhelm a concept. After you've developed a solid positioning and business plan, the design should flow quite naturally. Our big cautions: Don't hire a designer first. Many companies believe that the key to a new innovative concept is design—it's not. And be extremely cautious of design-of-the-year winning designs. They may win awards but they don't

win customers. Design processes should be as much about managing the customer experience and processing customers as they are about décor.

8. *Location, location, location.* Could any rule sound more like a clichébut at the same time be even more important now than ever? Countless concepts fail because they are put in the wrong place. They simply miss the mark in terms of where the target customer is, how far they are willing to drive, who the co-tenants should be, and the basic rules of access and visibility. Spend a lot of time and energy on getting the real estate right—it's not easy and particularly not easy today when the country has so many stores. The best (and most obvious) locations may now have price tags (rent) that are so prohibitive that it is difficult to make money even when hitting the projections. And green locations are just that—green and in this sense green means underdeveloped. They may work for large companies with patience, but make lousy proving grounds to test something new. For a new format, err on the side of overpaying—it is more critical to understand customer acceptance than it is to save a few dollars in the rent. And back to the previous business plan point, a good business plan should allow you to quickly gauge factors like rent sensitivity.

9. *Have great stuff to sell.* The best retail concepts are merchant and merchandise driven. They begin with a vision of what they want to sell and the function that merchandise delivers to a target customer. They

have an intuitive feel for trend—getting in, and out, at the right time. While customers may temporarily be mesmerized by a great marketing campaign, store design, or even a great salesperson, it is the product they buy, use, and ultimately remember. Whenever we put together a list of customer-driven attributes, whether it relates to great service or Greentailing, product always comes up at the top of the list. If you're beginning with something new, get the product right. And recognize that the process of hitting on the right product often takes time with plenty of trial and error along the way.

10. *Open strong but go slow.* This may sound a bit Confucius-like but there is wisdom in the logic. Open strong refers to gaining a boost of momentum when the doors open. Begin by opening at the right time of year when customer interest is at its highest. If you can't afford big marketing campaigns, do everything possible with friends, family, and cheap public relations to get the word out. Involve prominent people in the local community and other retail co-tenants to create buzz. Don't ignore the amazingly viral nature of the Internet and the use of online communities to spread the word. Grand opening events linked to causes is also a great way to create positive feelings.

Once opened, it is time to go slow. We have seen more businesses destroyed because of irrational expectations for fast growth and faulty time lines. Take the time to get the concept right. This could take months or even years to perfect. There are so many variables, from merchandise, pricing, sourcing, operations, and real estate that it is unrealistic to expect to get them all right from the starting gate.

11. *Roll out rationally.* We've heard it said that the hardest thing to do in retail is to open one store. The next hardest thing is to open a second location—and so on and so on. At each phase in expanding a concept, new skill sets and new resources come into play. At the early stages, a single hard-working entrepreneur can single-handedly drive a concept's success. As the concept expands, those skills need to be operationalized so others can learn from them. The dynamics of running an urban location versus a suburban location are often quite different. Opening outside a home market requires a retailer to have most of its program systematized because a broader span of control creates management challenges. You also lose your home-field advantage. A format that is well-understood intrinsically in its home market can struggle when heading somewhere new where it is relatively unknown. There are geographic differences in various regions around the United States and new and different competitors as well. And don't even get us started on the unique challenges of growing internationally and dealing with new cultures and new regulations. Each stage of growth requires retailers to assess how they go about doing business. While Wall Street is always enamored with growth

rates and how quickly retailers can expand, getting it right is always more important than going fast.

12. *Begin (and end) with passion!* Rational rules make sense on paper but they usually fail to capture the essence of real innovation and success versus another me-too idea. If we think back about the prior retail revolutions, they share a couple of common links. There was almost always an entrepreneur who was quick to develop (or recognize) a big idea. And, that entrepreneur was almost always considered to be a bit nutty and their ideas met with more than a little bit of skepticism. Small town Sam Walton fighting the giant retailers of his day. Howard Schultz trying to sell Americans an expensive cup of coffee. Jeff Bezos at Amazon selling millions of books online. Bernie Marcus and Arthur Blank creating a giant warehouse for home improvement products. Each of these innovators persevered because they had a deep passion for what they were doing and an abiding sense that they were doing the right thing. Time and again, passion wins out.

With years of experience observing and being part of new retail concept development, we feel strongly about this set of 12 rules. These rules hardly make it any easier, but they do define what will be necessary to be a successful retailer. And maybe create the next revolution. Rest assured, someone will.

CHAPTER FOURTEEN

LOOKING BACK AND LOOKING FORWARD

W e began this book by asking the question: What trends are in the marketplace that will revolutionize the retail industry? We know from experience that the only constant in retailing is change, and we can point to a multitude of new formats and new ideas that have fundamentally changed the retail landscape.

We showed that retailing will probably change even faster than ever as the life cycle for new concepts further compresses. Access to information, an increasingly diverse consumer, and global competition are all working together to ensure that the pace will not slow. And, the level of skills that retailers will need to succeed in the future is going to rise as well. Although a successful retailer must ultimately be best in at least one area, they are also going to have to be very good in a number of others as well. In other words, it is almost a prerequisite to be informed and on top of all major innovations.

We defined a revolutionary idea within the context of an *inflection point*—a moment in time where the business changes forever. Although it is sometimes hard to pinpoint that exact moment in time, we know empirically that the concept of an inflection point very much holds true for retailing. The complex interchange between a new retailer idea and other retailers' reactions keeps the market on its toes.

With the context set, we then went on to look in detail at some of the revolutionary ideas that are impacting the retail business now and well into the future. We began with a detailed discussion of Greentailing, the trend of the moment. We defined the concept of green, looked at its history, the consumer point of view, and a number of case studies of retailers putting green into action. We ended with a fairly concise set of action steps to address green within a retailer or supplier. While we instinctively knew that this trend was moving fast, we were blown away by just how fast. It is a living, breathing example of what happens when a concept reaches an inflection point. Green may have been in incubation for an awfully long time but it is an undeniable force of nature now. In the roughly 90 days that it took to write this book, we went back and rewrote the green chapters countless times. Even so, we openly acknowledge that many of the examples we cited will be obsolete by the time the book reaches publication. We're happy to see the Greentailing movement evolve so fast, but wish there would have been a little time to let the ink dry!

The other hot retail ideas chapters were a little more straightforward for us and on much more familiar ground:

- Demography and subsequent changes in consumer behavior represent the foundation of every significant retail innovation and will continue to do so in the future. And, the trends are a bit immutable—there are powerful forces at work that will ensure that the numbers won't change significantly.

- Experiential retailing is so exciting because it encapsulates what we hope is a movement away from low price as the be-all and end-all and the ascendancy of values and experiences to a more prominent place in the retail world. Of course, the growth of Greentailing and wellness is inexorably tied to the concept that experience-based retailing is valued by the consumer who is willing to pay a premium for the extra attention. Great experiential retailers represent the high art of retailing and demonstrate how exciting the retail business can be when executed at the highest level.

- The growth of nonstore retailing highlights another significant change in the retail world. While Internet retailing has notably received a lot of attention, retailers that utilize all available channels stand the best chance of maximizing their market potential. And there is going to be a number of new and highly creative ways to reach the consumer that no longer need to rely as heavily on bricks and mortar. The wired (and wireless) consumer can be reached in a number of ways.

- Service retailing is growing faster than traditional retailing and represents another revolution. While once viewed as an add-on, services may supplant products as the main driver of profit in retailers who learn to tap into customers' increasing need to have things done for them. Aging demographics combined with severe time compression is going to lead to a boom in service-related concepts.

- Brands going retail will have two key effects. One, they will continue to add to the ever-increasing competitive marketplace. And they will hasten the development of expanded skill sets on the part of retailer and supplier. Mastering an increasingly complex set of Ps will be the norm.

What did we miss? Plenty, we're sure. The focus on Greentailing somewhat obscures what we believe will be the monumental growth in all things involving wellness, which is a macro trend. Any and all innovations that concern anti-aging, weight management, sleep management, and health management are going to be rich sources of revolutionary innovation that will cut across all of our hot categories. Everyone is going to get into the act, from suppliers, to retailers, to new entrepreneurs. And the offers will be both store and nonstore products and services.

We stayed reasonably clear of technology innovation. For one, technology does not create a revolution in itself—it is an enabler for a future trend. And technology is a great place to be wrong, particularly as it relates to when it will be adopted.

There are dozens—literally—of promising technologies that guarantee to change retail, but we think they will mostly all move at slower rates than the projections we're seeing. They tend to be too focused on technology itself and not enough on the consumer and the problems that the technology will be solving for them.

The 12 rules of innovation provide some groundwork for developing a revolutionary retailing idea or concept, but creating something new is hardly a paint-by-numbers exercise. Real innovation typically comes from an inspired creator who has the passion to see it through in the face of many doubters.

It will take only a few years to see whether the concepts in this book will stand the test of time. Hopefully, we will be more right than wrong. In our now nearly 20-year-old newsletter on retailing called "Retail Watch," we have our own internal motto—*occasionally wrong but never in doubt!* And that is the spirit in which *Greentailing and Other Revolutions in Retailing* was written.

Notes

Preface

1. "You say you want a revolution ..." The Beatles, Lennon/McCartney, *Revolution* (SONY/ATV Music Publishing, 1968).

Chapter 2 Trends Are Interconnected

1. "It is not the strongest species ..." Attributed to Charles Darwin.

2. "I skate to where the puck ..." Attributed to Wayne Gretzky

Chapter 3 Greentailing 2.0—The Second Generation of Green

1. Earth-friendly products won't save the Earth if they don't save people money. Wal-Mart Advertisement

2. "No matter how sincere fashion designers ..." Eric Wilson and Paula Schwartz, "A World Consumed by Guilt," *New York Times*, December 17, 2007.

3. "In 2005, 68 percent of the world's 250 largest corporations ..." Olga Kharif, "Earth's Best Friend: Corporate America?," *BusinessWeek*, May 1, 2003; William Baue, "KPMG Finds More Than Half of Fortune 250 Issuing Standalone Sustainability Reports," *Sustainability Investment News*, June 22, 2005.

4. "Our children and grandchildren will be ..." Whole Foods Mission Statement web site: www.wholefoodsmarket.com

5. "The corporate roster ..." Claudia H. Deutsch, "Companies Giving Green an Office," *New York Times*, July 3, 2007.

Chapter 6 Putting Green Practices into Action

1. "Green is not a trend ..." Dan Butler, National Retail Federation, Vice President of Merchandising and Retail Operations.

2. "The Leadership in Energy and Environmental Design (LEED) ..." The U.S. Green Building Council, web site: www.usgbc.org.

3. "According to Swedish Furniture giant, Ikea ... " Ikea web site: www.ikea.com.

Chapter 11 Selling Services, Not Just Products

1. "According to the Convenient Care Association ..." Convenient Care Association, web site: www.convenient-careassociation.org.

Chapter 12 Brands Going Retail—The Battle for Control of the Customer

1. "Great brands will survive ..." Ted Zittel, McMillan|Doolittle affiliate.

Index